Hands-On Multi-Cloud Kubernetes

Multi-cluster kubernetes deployment and scaling with FluxCD, Virtual Kubelet, Submariner and KubeFed

Joe Brian

Published by: GitforGits
Publisher: Sonal Dhandre
www.gitforgits.com
support@gitforgits.com

Printed in India

First Printing: April 2023

ISBN: 978-8119177080

Cover Design by: Kitten Publishing

Content

Preface

"Hands-On Multi-Cloud Kubernetes" is an essential guide for anyone looking to gain a deep understanding of Kubernetes and how it can be used to manage multi-cloud infrastructure. With eight comprehensive chapters, this book provides hands-on experience in setting up Kubernetes clusters, administering deployments and updates, and working with AWS and GCP tools.

Readers will learn to work with a range of powerful tools, including Helm, FluxCD, Virtual Kubelet, Submariner, and KubeFed. With GitOps principles and workflows, they will practice continuous delivery and learn to manage secrets and config maps. They will build and deploy serverless clusters using Virtual Kubelet, and learn to scale them across multiple cloud environments. They will even be introduced to the world of cross-cluster networking with Submariner, where they will learn to perform service discovery, load balancing, and monitor networking metrics. Managing multi-cluster Kubernetes can be a daunting task, but with KubeFed, readers will gain the skills necessary to set up and deploy multicluster federation, making it easier than ever to administer their own infrastructure. And with multi-cloud CI/CD pipelines using Jenkins, they will perform end-to-end multi-cloud operations, ensuring their code is delivered quickly and efficiently.

Finally, the book covers security in Kubernetes, giving readers the tools and knowledge to configure RBAC, Kubernetes network policies, and secure data over Kubernetes clusters. They will even learn to use Open Policy Agent for managing compliance, ensuring that their infrastructure is both powerful and secure.

In this book you will learn how to:

- Learn Multi-cloud Kubernetes from fundamentals to advanced concepts and tools
- Setting up and managing Kubernetes clusters on multi-cloud infrastructure
- Working with powerful tools like Helm, FluxCD, and Virtual Kubelet
- Utilize Submariner for cross-cluster networking, service discovery, and load balancing
- CI/CD pipelines with Jenkins for end-to-end multi-cloud operations
- Practice GitOps principles and workflows for continuous delivery
- Building and deploying serverless clusters using Virtual Kubelet
- Managing multiple Kubernetes clusters as a single entity with KubeFed
- Security in Kubernetes with RBAC, network policies, and Open Policy Agent

Whether you are a beginner or an experienced practitioner, "Hands-On Multi-Cloud

Kubernetes" is an essential guide to understanding Kubernetes and managing multi-cloud infrastructure. With this book, readers will gain the knowledge and skills necessary to confidently take on any challenge that comes their way.

GitforGits

Prerequisites

This book is ideal for cloud professionals, devops team, kubernetes developer, networking professionals to explore multicloud networking, working with multi clusters, deployment of kubernetes and getting skilled with various innovative kubernetes tools. Knowing cloud networking or kubernetes is sufficient to begin with the book.

Codes Usage

Are you in need of some helpful code examples to assist you in your programming and documentation? Look no further! Our book offers a wealth of supplemental material, including code examples and exercises.

Not only is this book here to aid you in getting your job done, but you have our permission to use the example code in your programs and documentation. However, please note that if you are reproducing a significant portion of the code, we do require you to contact us for permission.

But don't worry, using several chunks of code from this book in your program or answering a question by citing our book and quoting example code does not require permission. But if you do choose to give credit, an attribution typically includes the title, author, publisher, and ISBN. For example, "Hands-On Multi-Cloud Kubernetes by Joe Brian".

If you are unsure whether your intended use of the code examples falls under fair use or the permissions outlined above, please do not hesitate to reach out to us at: kittenpub.kdp@gmail.com.

We are happy to assist and clarify any concerns.

Acknowledgement

I owe a tremendous debt of gratitude to Pravin Dhandre, my editor, for his unflagging enthusiasm and wise counsel throughout the entire process of writing this book. His knowledge and careful editing helped make sure the piece was useful for people of all reading levels and comprehension skills. In addition, I'd like to thank everyone involved in the publishing process for their efforts in making this book a reality. Their efforts, from copyediting to advertising, made the project what it is today.

Finally, I'd like to express my gratitude to everyone who has shown me unconditional love and encouragement throughout my life. Their support was crucial to the completion of this book. I appreciate your help with this endeavour and your continued interest in my career.

Chapter 1: Introduction to Multi-cloud Kubernetes

Evolution of Multi-cloud

Cloud computing has become popular among businesses due to its ability to offer flexible and readily available computing resources. Traditionally, companies used a single cloud provider to meet their infrastructure needs. However, with the advancements in cloud technology, multi-cloud strategies have emerged as a promising alternative. This section aims to introduce the evolution of multi-cloud and discuss the challenges that arise from multi-cloud Kubernetes deployments for cloud professionals.

Initially, companies relied on a single cloud provider to provide computing resources, and it served them well. However, as cloud technology advanced, businesses began to demand more flexibility, better pricing, and improved service quality. As a result, multi-cloud strategies emerged, which involve using multiple cloud providers to distribute workload and minimize downtime. However, multi-cloud deployment is not without its challenges. One of the primary difficulties is managing Kubernetes clusters across different cloud providers. Kubernetes is an open-source platform used for container orchestration, and it helps manage and automate containerized applications. But deploying Kubernetes clusters across multiple cloud providers can be complex and time-consuming.

Early Days of Cloud Computing

During the inception of cloud computing, three dominant cloud providers, namely Amazon Web Services (AWS), Microsoft Azure, and Google Cloud Platform (GCP), emerged, providing various services including Infrastructure as a Service (IaaS), Platform as a Service (PaaS), and Software as a Service (SaaS). These solutions have been beneficial for businesses as they can outsource their IT infrastructure and concentrate on their core competencies, making it easier for them to operate. With IaaS, businesses can rent virtualized computing resources and storage, while PaaS offers an environment for building, testing, and deploying software applications without requiring complex infrastructure setup. SaaS provides access to software applications on a subscription basis, eliminating the need for costly licensing and maintenance fees. These cloud services have enabled businesses to reduce their capital expenditure, improved scalability, and enhanced flexibility, making it easier for them to focus on their core activities. The rapid growth of cloud computing has led to the emergence of more providers, each offering unique services, further widening the options available to businesses.

Emergence of Multi-cloud

With the increasing adoption of cloud services, businesses have become aware of the risks associated with relying on a single provider. This includes being locked into a specific vendor's platform, which may lead to limited flexibility and increased costs in the long run.

In response to this challenge, many companies have begun to adopt a multi-cloud strategy, which involves using multiple cloud providers to meet their computing needs.

The emergence of multi-cloud has several benefits for organizations, including improved redundancy, cost optimization, and the ability to leverage the unique strengths of each provider. By using multiple cloud providers, companies can distribute their workloads across different providers and reduce the risk of downtime. This helps to ensure business continuity, as even if one provider experiences an outage, the others can continue to operate. Another advantage of multi-cloud is cost optimization. By using different providers for different workloads, organizations can choose the most cost-effective option for each workload, rather than being locked into a single provider's pricing model. This can lead to significant cost savings over time. Furthermore, multi-cloud enables companies to leverage the unique strengths of each provider. Different providers may excel in different areas, such as security, scalability, or machine learning. By using multiple providers, organizations can choose the provider that best meets their specific needs for each workload.

Kubernetes and Containerization

Around the same time, containerization technology emerged as a popular method for packaging and deploying applications. Containers are lightweight and can be easily moved, which makes them a great choice for building and deploying applications in a cloud-native environment. Kubernetes is an open-source platform for container orchestration, which rapidly became the preferred solution for managing containerized applications at scale.

Containerization technology has gained a lot of traction in recent years due to the advantages it provides for application development and deployment. Containers are a lightweight alternative to traditional virtual machines and can be easily moved between different environments, making them a popular choice for cloud-native development. The use of containers also allows for more efficient resource utilization, as multiple containers can be run on the same host, making it an ideal solution for scaling applications horizontally.

Kubernetes is an open-source platform that has emerged as the standard for container orchestration. It simplifies the management of containerized applications, allowing developers to easily deploy, scale, and manage them in a cluster. Kubernetes also provides features such as load balancing, service discovery, and automated rollouts and rollbacks, which help to ensure that applications are highly available and reliable. As a result, Kubernetes has become a vital tool in the modern DevOps toolkit, enabling organizations to deliver applications faster and with greater reliability.

The Rise of Multi-cloud Kubernetes

With the growing popularity of multi-cloud strategies, organizations face the challenge of managing containerized applications across various cloud providers. In response, Kubernetes has emerged as an ideal solution since it is provider-agnostic, allowing it to operate on any cloud infrastructure. Consequently, multi-cloud Kubernetes deployments are on the rise, enabling organizations to deploy their containerized applications on multiple cloud platforms while using a single control plane to manage them.

Additionally, Kubernetes provides a consistent and standard way of managing containers, making it easier for developers to deploy and manage their applications across multiple cloud platforms. With the advent of multi-cloud Kubernetes deployments, organizations can enjoy the flexibility of running their containerized applications on different cloud providers. Moreover, by using a single control plane to manage their deployments, organizations can simplify their operations, reduce costs, and improve their overall efficiency. Therefore, Kubernetes has become a critical technology for organizations adopting multi-cloud strategies.

Challenges for Cloud Professionals

Installations of Kubernetes across multiple clouds present cloud professionals with a new set of challenges. The following are the ones:

- Managing a Kubernetes deployment that spans multiple clouds can be difficult because doing so requires in-depth familiarity with the infrastructure, services, and configurations offered by each individual cloud provider.
- The use of virtual private networks (VPNs), load balancers, and ingress controllers are just some of the advanced networking configurations that are required to guarantee uninterrupted communication between applications that are running on different cloud platforms.
- Securing a multi-cloud Kubernetes deployment requires the management of security policies and access controls across multiple cloud providers. This can be a difficult and time-consuming process.
- Monitoring and optimizing costs in a multi-cloud environment can be challenging due to the fact that each cloud provider uses their own pricing model and billing structure.
- Ensuring compliance with data protection regulations such as GDPR and HIPAA can be difficult in a multi-cloud environment because data may be stored and processed in multiple locations with varying levels of security. This can make it difficult to ensure compliance with these regulations.

Overcoming Challenges

Cloud professionals face numerous challenges in their day-to-day operations. One of the main obstacles is the ever-changing nature of cloud technology. To conquer these difficulties, it is essential for cloud experts to acquire an in-depth knowledge of each cloud provider's services, tools, and best practices. In addition, they must continuously learn and enhance their skills to keep pace with the latest advancements in Kubernetes and multi-cloud technologies.

To ensure that cloud professionals have a comprehensive understanding of the services and tools offered by cloud providers, they must undertake thorough training programs. This will equip them with the necessary knowledge to evaluate which tools are suitable for a particular use case. Additionally, they must stay abreast of the latest trends and developments in the field by attending industry conferences, engaging with peers and experts, and participating in online forums. By investing in continuous learning and upskilling, cloud professionals can ensure that they have the necessary expertise to address the challenges presented by the dynamic cloud technology landscape.

Some strategies for addressing these challenges include:

- Standardizing deployment processes and configurations across different cloud providers can help ensure consistency and facilitate easier management. Additionally, leveraging automation tools such as Infrastructure as Code (IaC) and Continuous Integration/Continuous Deployment (CI/CD) pipelines can streamline deployment and management tasks.
- Another crucial practice is implementing a centralized monitoring and logging solution that can provide visibility into the performance and health of applications running across multiple cloud platforms. By doing so, it becomes easier to detect and resolve issues that may arise.
- In a multi-cloud environment, security risks may be greater. Therefore, it is important to adopt security best practices such as the principle of least privilege, encryption, and proper access controls to mitigate these risks. It is also essential to use cost management tools and services provided by cloud providers or third-party solutions to monitor and optimize costs across multiple clouds.
- Finally, regular compliance audits and assessments can help ensure that multi-cloud deployments meet necessary data protection and regulatory requirements. By conducting such audits, organizations can identify and address any compliance issues that may arise.

Future of Multi-cloud Kubernetes

As organizations continue to adopt multi-cloud strategies and embrace Kubernetes, the demand for skilled cloud professionals will grow. The future of multi-cloud Kubernetes will likely involve further abstraction of cloud services, simplifying the management of multi-cloud deployments and reducing the complexity for cloud professionals.

Additionally, emerging technologies, such as edge computing and serverless architectures, will continue to shape the multi-cloud landscape, presenting new challenges and opportunities for cloud professionals. The evolution of multi-cloud and the adoption of Kubernetes have transformed the way organizations manage their IT infrastructure. Multi-cloud Kubernetes deployments present a new set of challenges for cloud professionals, requiring them to develop a deep understanding of multiple cloud platforms and continuously adapt to new technologies. By embracing these challenges and investing in continuous learning, cloud professionals can position themselves for success in the ever-evolving world of cloud computing.

Benefits and Challenges of Multi-cloud Deployments

Multi-cloud deployments have gained traction in recent times due to the flexibility and scalability they offer. With multiple cloud service providers at their disposal, organizations can distribute their workload efficiently, avoid vendor lock-in, and ensure high availability of their applications. Additionally, they can leverage the unique features of each cloud platform to optimize their operations and reduce costs. However, multi-cloud deployments also pose certain challenges, such as the complexity of managing multiple vendors and ensuring data security across different cloud environments. Organizations need to adopt robust management and security practices to overcome these challenges and fully realize the benefits of multi-cloud deployments. In this section, we delve deeper into the benefits and challenges of multi-cloud deployments in the current scenario.

Benefits of Multi-cloud Deployments

Flexibility and Agility: Multi-cloud deployments provide organizations with unrivaled flexibility and agility, enabling them to pick and choose the best services and features offered by various cloud providers to meet the specific requirements of their business. This flexibility can lead to faster innovation as well as improved responsiveness to the constantly shifting demands of the market.

Cost Optimization: Organizations are able to optimize costs by selecting the most cost-effective services and pricing models by leveraging multiple cloud providers, which enables them to leverage multiple cloud providers. They can also benefit from the price competition that exists between cloud providers by using it to their advantage to negotiate better rates and discounts.

Improved Reliability and Redundancy: Multi-cloud deployments offer increased reliability and redundancy by distributing applications and workloads across multiple cloud providers. This results in increased reliability and redundancy for the overall system. This strategy helps reduce the likelihood of downtime or data loss brought on by issues with the infrastructure, such as provider outages, failed hardware, or other problems.

Enhanced Performance: Organizations that use multi-cloud deployments have the ability to more strategically choose cloud providers that have data centers located in close proximity to their users. This helps to reduce latency and improves the overall performance of applications.

Risk Mitigation: Relying on a single cloud provider can lead to vendor lock-in, which makes it difficult for businesses to switch cloud providers or relocate applications back on-premises if they are required to do so. Multi-cloud deployments reduce the severity of this risk because they ensure that data and applications are not dependent on a single service provider.

Compliance and Data Sovereignty: There are circumstances in which regulatory requirements or laws concerning data sovereignty require that data be stored and processed within particular geographical boundaries. Multi-cloud deployments give businesses the ability to fulfill these prerequisites by selecting cloud service providers who have data centers situated in the necessary geographic areas.

Challenges of Multi-cloud Deployments

Increased Complexity: The management of a multi-cloud environment can be difficult for organizations because it requires them to work with a variety of different provider interfaces, application programming interfaces (APIs), tools, and configurations. Because of the increased complexity, operational costs may go up, and the learning curve for IT staff may become more challenging.

Data Management: The management of data can be difficult because it can be difficult to guarantee data consistency, security, and accessibility when using multiple cloud providers. In order for organizations to keep their data available and intact, they need to implement effective data management strategies. Some examples of these strategies include data synchronization, backup, and recovery procedures.

Security and Compliance: The need for organizations to manage security policies, access controls, and encryption standards across multiple cloud environments can make security and compliance efforts more difficult to manage when multi-cloud deployments are utilized. In order to stay in compliance with the industry's regulations, this can be a time-consuming process that might call for additional resources.

Networking and Connectivity: It can be difficult to set up a connection that is both safe and dependable between applications and services that are running in different cloud environments. To ensure uninterrupted communication between workloads that are running on different cloud platforms, businesses need to design and implement networking solutions such as virtual private networks (VPNs), direct connections (Direct Connect), and express routes (ExpressRoute).

Expertise and Capabilities: In order to manage multi-cloud deployments effectively, IT professionals need to have a comprehensive understanding of the services, tools, and best practices offered by each cloud provider. As a consequence of this, businesses may find that they need to make additional investments in training and certification programs for their IT staff in order to guarantee that they have the necessary skills to effectively manage multi-cloud environments.

Management of Costs: Although multi-cloud deployments can assist organizations in optimizing costs, it can be difficult to manage and monitor expenses across multiple cloud providers. Cost management is an important aspect of multi-cloud deployments. In order to keep a handle on their spending across multiple clouds, businesses need to put in place appropriate cost management procedures and make use of appropriate cost management tools, such as cost calculators and third-party cost management solutions.

In summary, adopting multi-cloud deployments can bring several advantages, including enhanced flexibility, cost efficiency, and better dependability. Nonetheless, it is crucial for organizations to thoughtfully examine the obstacles linked with managing several cloud environments, such as heightened intricacy, data administration, and security risks. By comprehending these challenges, organizations can devise an effective plan to handle their multi-cloud infrastructure efficiently. It is also essential to ensure that the organization's IT team is equipped with the necessary knowledge and expertise to manage various cloud platforms. Moreover, businesses need to implement appropriate tools and strategies to manage their multi-cloud environments efficiently. Proper planning and execution can help organizations harness the benefits of multi-cloud deployments while mitigating potential risks and challenges associated with it.

Key Concepts: Clusters, Nodes, and Namespaces

To effectively manage multi-cloud Kubernetes deployments, it is essential to understand some key concepts, including Clusters, Nodes, and Namespaces. In this section, we will explain these concepts in detail and introduce a few other essential components to help you better understand Kubernetes.

Clusters

A Kubernetes environment can't function without a cluster as its backbone. It is a collection of computers, also known as nodes, that collaborate with one another to offer a unified platform for the execution of containerized applications. Multiple nodes, which may be either physical or virtual and may be located either on-premises or in the cloud, make up a cluster.

Clusters grant you the ability to manage and scale your applications in accordance with the requirements of those applications, automatically handling tasks such as load balancing, scaling, and updates. The following are the primary constituents of a cluster:

Control Plane

The control plane is a collection of components that are responsible for managing the cluster's overall state. It incorporates the Kubernetes API server, etcd, which is a distributed key-value store, in addition to various other components such as the controller manager and scheduler.

Nodes

The worker computers known as nodes are the ones that are responsible for running containerized applications. Each node that makes up a cluster is responsible for running a container runtime (like Docker), as well as the Kubernetes agent known as kubelet.

Nodes

Nodes are the individual machines, either physical or virtual, that make up a Kubernetes cluster. They host the containerized applications and workloads. Nodes can be organized into groups or "pools" based on their resources, such as CPU, memory, and storage. There are two types of nodes:

Worker Nodes

Worker nodes are integral parts of a distributed system responsible for executing containerized workloads and applications. These nodes execute a container runtime such as Docker and the kubelet agent. The kubelet agent connects to the control plane to ensure that containers are running optimally. The control plane is a critical component of Kubernetes, responsible for managing and monitoring the overall health of the cluster. In particular, the kubelet agent is responsible for executing instructions from the control plane and ensuring that the containers are running as expected. This communication between the control plane and worker nodes is essential to guarantee that the system operates smoothly and efficiently.

Master Nodes

In a Kubernetes cluster, the control plane is managed by master nodes, which oversee the state of the entire cluster and facilitate communication between worker nodes. The key components of the control plane, such as the API server, etcd, controller manager, and scheduler, run on these master nodes. These components work together to ensure the smooth operation of the Kubernetes cluster. For instance, the API server serves as the primary interface for cluster management, while etcd provides a distributed key-value store for storing configuration data. The controller manager ensures that the desired state of the cluster matches the actual state, while the scheduler is responsible for assigning workloads to appropriate worker nodes.

Namespaces

Namespaces are a way to organize and separate resources within a Kubernetes cluster. They provide a virtual boundary for grouping and isolating resources, such as pods, services, and deployments. Namespaces are particularly useful in multi-tenant environments, where multiple teams or projects share the same cluster.

A few examples of common applications for namespaces are as follows:
- Allocating Resources: You can ensure that there is a fair distribution of resources among the various teams or projects that are sharing the cluster by allocating resources (such as CPU and memory) to specific namespaces.
- Access Control: Namespaces give users the ability to implement role-based access control (RBAC), which in turn gives users the ability to restrict access to particular resources contained within a namespace.
- The use of namespaces allows you to create distinct environments for development, testing, and production within a single cluster. This helps to prevent conflicts and maintain isolation.

Pods

The pod in Kubernetes is the smallest and most basic unit in the system. It is possible for it to hold one or more containers and it represents a single instance of a process that is currently running. The requirements of an application will determine whether a pod should be automatically created, scaled, or deleted. Pods are ephemeral and have these capabilities.

Services

Services are a means by which applications that are running in pods can be exposed to the network, either internally or externally to the cluster. They offer a consistent IP address as well as a DNS name, which makes it possible for various application components to communicate with one another.

Deployments

Deployments are a high-level abstraction that allow you to manage the desired state of your applications in a declarative manner. Deployments are also known as deployments. They contribute to the management of the pod lifecycle by ensuring that the required number of replicas is operational and automatically rolling out updates or rolling back changes as required.

ConfigMaps and Secrets

ConfigMaps and Secrets are used to store configuration data and sensitive information, respectively, that can be shared across multiple pods. ConfigMaps are used to store configuration data. Secrets are used to store sensitive information. Because of this, you are able to decouple configuration data from container images, which makes it much simpler to update and manage application configurations without having to rebuild container images.

Ingress

Ingress is a Kubernetes resource that manages how users from the outside world can connect to the services that are running inside of a cluster. It gives you the ability to define rules for directing HTTP and HTTPS traffic to the appropriate services based on criteria such as the host or path of the request.

Persistent Storage

Persistent storage is an essential component of many applications because it enables data to be stored and accessed across multiple pods and even after the lifecycle of a pod has expired. This makes persistent storage an indispensable part of many applications. Persistent Volumes (PV), Persistent Volume Claims (PVC), and Storage Classes are some examples of the different kinds of persistent storage solutions that Kubernetes is able to support.

Resource Quotas

A namespace's ability to use resources like a computer's processing power, memory, and storage space can be constrained by setting a resource quota for the namespace. This prevents any one namespace from consuming an excessive amount of resources and guarantees that resources are distributed fairly among the various groups or projects that share the same cluster.

Horizontal Pod Autoscaler (HPA)

It is a feature of Kubernetes that automatically scales the number of pod replicas based on metrics such as CPU utilization or custom metricss. HPA is an abbreviation for Horizontal Pod Autoscaler. This helps ensure that applications are able to handle varying traffic loads while simultaneously optimizing their use of available resources.

Custom Resource Definitions (CRDs)

Custom Resource Definitions, also known as CRDs, give you the ability to extend the functionality of the Kubernetes API by defining new types of custom resources. Because of this, you will have the ability to create and manage custom resources that are unique to your applications, just like you can do with built-in Kubernetes resources such as pods and services.

You will be in a better position to manage and optimize Kubernetes deployments across multiple clouds if you have a solid understanding of these key concepts. You will be able to construct and manage complex applications that are scalable across multiple cloud environments as you gain more experience working with Kubernetes and develop a deeper understanding of these concepts and their interactions.

Understanding Multi-cloud and Multi-cluster Architectures

Multi-cloud architecture refers to a deployment model that involves using multiple cloud providers to meet an organization's computing needs. Multi-cloud architecture allows organizations to take advantage of the unique strengths of each cloud provider while minimizing the risks of vendor lock-in, downtime, and data loss.

There are several different multi-cloud architectures that organizations can choose from, each with its own strengths and weaknesses. In this section, we will describe some of the most common multi-cloud architectures and their characteristics.

Hub and Spoke Architecture

The hub and spoke architecture is a common multi-cloud architecture that involves a central hub, which acts as a control plane, and multiple spokes, which are cloud providers that provide compute, storage, and networking resources. The central hub manages and orchestrates workloads across multiple cloud providers, enabling organizations to leverage the strengths of each provider.

The advantages of the hub and spoke architecture include:

Centralized Control: The central hub provides a single point of control for managing and orchestrating workloads across multiple cloud providers.

Improved Security: The central hub provides a layer of security between the spokes, isolating them from one another and reducing the risk of data breaches and unauthorized access.

Simplified Operations: By centralizing operations, organizations can simplify management tasks like security, networking, and cost optimization.

Mesh Architecture

The mesh architecture is a decentralized multi-cloud architecture that involves multiple cloud providers, each acting as an equal node in the network. In this architecture, there is no central hub, and workloads can be run on any cloud provider, depending on availability and performance.

The advantages of the mesh architecture include:

Increased Resilience: By leveraging multiple cloud providers, organizations can improve application resilience and uptime, as workloads can be shifted between providers based on availability and performance.

Improved Flexibility: The mesh architecture allows organizations to deploy workloads on any cloud provider, enabling them to choose the provider that best meets their needs at any given time.

Reduced Risk of Vendor Lock-in: With no central hub, the mesh architecture reduces the risk of vendor lock-in, enabling organizations to switch cloud providers as needed.

Hybrid Cloud Architecture

Hybrid cloud architecture is a multi-cloud architecture that combines public cloud providers with private cloud or on-premises infrastructure. In this architecture, organizations can leverage public cloud providers for scalability and flexibility while retaining control over sensitive data and workloads.

The advantages of the hybrid cloud architecture include:

Improved Security: By retaining sensitive data and workloads in a private cloud or on-premises infrastructure, organizations can improve security and compliance.

Increased Flexibility: The hybrid cloud architecture allows organizations to take advantage of the scalability and flexibility of public cloud providers while retaining control over sensitive data.

Cost Optimization: The hybrid cloud architecture enables organizations to optimize costs by leveraging public cloud providers for non-sensitive workloads and retaining private cloud or on-premises infrastructure for sensitive data and workloads.

Multi-cloud Federation

Multi-cloud federation is a multi-cloud architecture that involves the coordination of multiple cloud providers to provide a unified computing platform. In this architecture, multiple cloud providers are managed as a single entity, enabling organizations to leverage the strengths of each provider while minimizing complexity.

The advantages of multi-cloud federation include:

Improved Flexibility: Multi-cloud federation allows organizations to choose the best cloud provider for each workload based on factors like cost, performance, and availability.

Simplified Operations: Multi-cloud federation simplifies management tasks by providing a single management interface for multiple cloud providers.

Improved Resilience: By leveraging multiple cloud providers, multi-cloud federation can improve application resilience and uptime.

Overall, organizations must carefully consider the advantages and disadvantages of different multi-cloud architectures before deciding which approach to adopt. By selecting the right multi-cloud architecture for their needs, organizations can leverage the unique strengths of each cloud provider while minimizing the risks and complexity of managing multiple cloud environments.

Prerequisites and Tools

To learn multi-cloud Kubernetes, it's important to have a solid foundation in several key concepts and tools. These include Kubernetes basics, containerization, cloud providers, networking, DevOps practices, monitoring and logging, cloud-native tools, and multi-cloud concepts.

Kubernetes Basics

Kubernetes is an open-source container orchestration system that automates the deployment, scaling, and management of containerized applications. It allows you to manage containers as a group rather than as individual entities, enabling you to deploy and manage applications more efficiently.

To get started with Kubernetes, you should have a good understanding of the basics, including how to create and manage pods, services, and deployments. You should also be familiar with Kubernetes resources such as ConfigMaps, Secrets, and Ingress. Understanding these concepts will help you deploy and manage your applications on Kubernetes more efficiently.

Containerization

Containerization is the process of packaging an application and its dependencies into a single container image. Containers provide a lightweight, portable way to run applications across different environments, making it easier to deploy and manage them.
To learn multi-cloud Kubernetes, you should have a strong grasp of containerization and how it works. You should be familiar with container runtimes such as Docker and container orchestration tools like Kubernetes. This knowledge will help you containerize your applications and deploy them to Kubernetes more easily.

Cloud Providers

Multi-cloud Kubernetes involves using multiple cloud providers to meet your computing needs. To get started, you should have a basic understanding of the cloud providers you plan to use, including their strengths and weaknesses, pricing models, and how to create and manage resources on their platforms.

Different cloud providers have different strengths and weaknesses, and understanding these will help you choose the right provider for your workload. You should also be familiar with the different resource types provided by each provider, such as compute, storage, and networking resources.

Networking

Networking is a critical component of Kubernetes, and you should have a solid understanding of networking concepts such as service discovery, load balancing, and network policies. Kubernetes provides several networking primitives, such as Services and Ingress, to help you manage network traffic between your application components.

To learn multi-cloud Kubernetes, you should also understand how networking works across different cloud providers. Each cloud provider has its own networking model, and understanding these models will help you configure and manage networking across multiple cloud providers more efficiently.

DevOps Practices

DevOps practices are essential for managing Kubernetes environments. You should have a good understanding of continuous integration and deployment (CI/CD), version control, and infrastructure as code (IaC). These practices help you automate and streamline the deployment and management of your applications.

To learn multi-cloud Kubernetes, you should also understand how DevOps practices can be used to manage Kubernetes environments across multiple cloud providers. This includes using version control to manage Kubernetes manifests, using IaC to automate infrastructure provisioning, and using CI/CD pipelines to automate application deployment.

Monitoring and Logging

Monitoring and logging are essential for maintaining the health and availability of your Kubernetes environment. Kubernetes provides several built-in tools for monitoring and logging, such as Metrics Server and the Kubernetes Dashboard. You should also be familiar with tools for monitoring and logging Kubernetes clusters and applications, such as Prometheus and Grafana.

To learn multi-cloud Kubernetes, you should understand how to monitor and log your applications across multiple cloud providers. This includes using centralized logging and monitoring tools to collect and analyze data from multiple environments.

Cloud Native Tools

Cloud-native tools and technologies are designed to work with Kubernetes and other cloud-native technologies. These tools help you manage and orchestrate your Kubernetes environment more efficiently. Examples of cloud-native tools include Istio, which provides service mesh functionality, and Kubernetes Operations (Kops), which provides a toolset for managing Kubernetes clusters in production.

To learn multi-cloud Kubernetes, you should be familiar with cloud-native tools and technologies, including tools for service mesh, such as Istio, and tools for running Kubernetes in production, such as Kops. Understanding these tools will help you manage and optimize your Kubernetes environment across multiple cloud providers.

Multi-cloud Concepts

Multi-cloud concepts are essential for understanding how to deploy and manage Kubernetes across multiple cloud providers. These concepts include understanding how to choose the right cloud providers for your workload, how to manage multiple cloud providers, and how to optimize costs and performance in a multi-cloud environment.

To learn multi-cloud Kubernetes, you should be familiar with these concepts and understand how to apply them to your Kubernetes environment. This includes understanding how to manage different cloud providers using a single management plane, how to optimize costs by using the right cloud provider for each workload, and how to ensure high availability and performance across multiple cloud providers.

Overall, to learn multi-cloud Kubernetes, you should have a strong foundation in several key concepts and tools, including Kubernetes basics, containerization, cloud providers, networking, DevOps practices, monitoring and logging, cloud-native tools, and multi-cloud concepts. By understanding these concepts and tools, you will be better equipped to deploy and manage your Kubernetes workloads across multiple cloud providers, ensuring high availability, scalability, and cost optimization.

Setting Stage for Multi-cloud Kubernetes

To implement a multi-cloud Kubernetes strategy, it's crucial to ensure that your environment and infrastructure are ready to support the deployment of Kubernetes across various cloud providers. This requires thorough preparation, including setting up the necessary resources and configurations, such as networking, security, and storage, to ensure seamless operations across different clouds. In essence, multi-cloud Kubernetes is about creating a unified system that enables you to harness the benefits of multiple clouds while avoiding vendor lock-in and achieving greater flexibility, scalability, and resiliency. By taking the time to prepare your environment and infrastructure, you can lay the foundation for a successful multi-cloud Kubernetes deployment.

The following steps can be used as a standard procedure to help you set the stage for multi-cloud Kubernetes.

Define Requirements

To pave the way for multi-cloud Kubernetes, the initial measure is to establish your specifications. This encompasses comprehending your workload requisites, financial plan, and the preferred degree of jurisdiction over your surroundings. It is crucial to define your requirements before migrating to multi-cloud Kubernetes to ensure a seamless transition and optimized performance. By identifying these parameters, you can efficiently allocate resources and select the appropriate service providers to fulfill your needs. Additionally, understanding your budget and desired level of control can help avoid unexpected expenses and ensure the proper level of oversight.

Choose Cloud Providers

After outlining your requirements, the subsequent step involves selecting the cloud providers that meet your criteria. Your decision should be based on factors such as workload demands, financial constraints, and the features and pricing plans provided by each supplier. The ideal approach is to assess each provider's suitability to ensure that you pick the one that can best meet your requirements while remaining within your budget. Therefore, selecting a cloud provider should be a deliberate process that takes into account multiple factors, including your specific needs and the characteristics of each provider's services.

Choose Kubernetes Distribution

After deciding to use Kubernetes, the next crucial step is selecting the appropriate distribution. It should be selected based on the workload requirements and the desired degree of control over the environment. It's also important to evaluate if the distribution facilitates running Kubernetes on various cloud providers. Therefore, carefully considering these factors can help to determine the best-suited Kubernetes distribution for your needs.

Plan Infrastructure

Once you have chosen your cloud providers and Kubernetes distribution, the next step is to plan your infrastructure. This includes:

Provisioning your cloud resources

You will need to create the compute, storage, and networking resources needed to run your Kubernetes environment on each cloud provider.

Configuring your networking

You will need to configure your networking to enable communication between your Kubernetes clusters on different cloud providers.

Install and Configure Kubernetes

The next step is to install and configure Kubernetes on each cloud provider. This typically involves using tools like kubeadm or kops to set up the cluster. You should also configure your Kubernetes clusters to work across multiple cloud providers.

Set Up Multi-cloud Management Tools

After successfully deploying your Kubernetes clusters, the subsequent crucial step is to configure multi-cloud management tools that enable you to manage and orchestrate your Kubernetes environment across several cloud providers. Various widely used tools are available such as Istio, KubeDirector, and Terraform, that can help you to streamline your Kubernetes deployment and management across different cloud platforms. These tools offer valuable features such as enhanced scalability, security, and automation, enabling you to efficiently manage and control your Kubernetes environment, irrespective of the cloud provider you use.

Deploy and Manage Applications

The final step is to deploy and manage your applications on your multi-cloud Kubernetes environment. This typically involves creating Kubernetes manifests that define the resources needed to run your application, such as pods, services, and deployments. You can use tools like Helm to help you manage the deployment of your applications.

Overall, setting the stage for multi-cloud Kubernetes requires careful planning and execution. By following the steps outlined above, you can create a scalable and flexible Kubernetes environment that meets your workload needs and budget.

Summary

In recent years, there has been a significant shift towards multi cloud environments, where organizations utilize multiple cloud providers to meet their computing needs. Multi cloud Kubernetes has emerged as a popular solution for managing these complex environments.

One of the key benefits of multi cloud deployments is that it allows organizations to avoid vendor lock-in and take advantage of the unique capabilities of different cloud providers. Multi cloud Kubernetes enables organizations to manage their applications and services across multiple cloud platforms seamlessly. However, there are also several challenges associated with multi cloud deployments. One major challenge is ensuring consistent security and compliance across multiple environments. Another challenge is managing the complexity of deploying and configuring applications across multiple clouds.

To address these challenges, multi cloud Kubernetes utilizes key concepts such as clusters, nodes, and namespaces. Clusters are a collection of nodes that work together to provide computing resources for running applications. Nodes are individual machines that make up a cluster, such as virtual machines or physical servers. Namespaces are virtual clusters within a physical cluster that allow for logical separation of resources and policies.

Multi cloud Kubernetes architectures can be categorized into two types: centralized and decentralized. In a centralized architecture, a single control plane manages multiple clusters across multiple clouds. In contrast, a decentralized architecture involves multiple control planes, each managing a single cluster.

Setting the stage for multi cloud deployments involves several steps. First, organizations need to define their objectives and identify the cloud providers that best meet their needs. Next, they need to establish a multi cloud strategy and determine the appropriate architecture. Once the strategy is in place, organizations can begin building and configuring their multi cloud Kubernetes clusters. Ongoing monitoring and management are also critical to ensure the success of multi cloud deployments.

In summary, multi cloud Kubernetes has emerged as a powerful solution for managing complex multi cloud environments. While it offers many benefits, it also presents unique challenges that organizations must navigate. Key concepts such as clusters, nodes, and namespaces are essential to managing multi cloud deployments, and organizations must carefully consider their architecture and strategy to ensure success.

CHAPTER 2: KUBERNETES CLUSTER MANAGEMENT AND DEPLOYMENT

Setting Up Kubernetes Cluster

Creating a multi-cloud Kubernetes cluster can offer several benefits, including increased availability, redundancy, and flexibility. This section will walk you through the process of setting up a multi-cloud Kubernetes cluster using AWS and GCP, two popular cloud providers. We will be utilizing kubeadm to create the cluster and Kops to manage it. However, this book assumes that you have already established the necessary infrastructure and have credentials for both providers.

By utilizing two different cloud providers, we can reduce the risk of downtime and potential data loss. This setup also allows for the distribution of workloads across multiple cloud platforms to optimize resource usage. To successfully complete this task, you will need a basic understanding of Kubernetes, AWS, and GCP. Additionally, you should have prior experience setting up infrastructure on both cloud providers. With the necessary prerequisites in place, we can now begin the process of setting up our multi-cloud Kubernetes cluster.

Install Prerequisites

To utilize Kubernetes, you must install several tools. The Kubernetes CLI tool, kubectl, is necessary for managing and deploying applications on the cluster. Additionally, you'll need kubeadm, a Kubernetes cluster bootstrapping tool that simplifies the creation of a new Kubernetes cluster. Kops, another essential tool, is used to operate Kubernetes clusters on Amazon Web Services (AWS). AWS CLI, a command-line interface for AWS services, is also required to configure and manage Kubernetes clusters on AWS. Similarly, the Google Cloud SDK, a command-line tool, is necessary to manage and deploy Kubernetes clusters on Google Cloud. By installing and utilizing these tools, you can efficiently deploy and manage your Kubernetes cluster, making it easier to build, deploy, and scale your applications.

[Note: Please follow the official documentation for installing these tools for your specific operating system.]

Configure AWS and GCP Credentials

After installing the AWS CLI and Google Cloud SDK, you need to configure the credentials for both providers. To do this, follow the official documentation for configuring the AWS CLI and configuring the Google Cloud SDK.

Create Kubernetes Cluster Specification

With Kops, we can create a cluster specification (a manifest in YAML format) that describes our desired cluster configuration. Let us create a sample specification:

```yaml
apiVersion: kops.k8s.io/v1alpha2
kind: Cluster
metadata:
  name: my-multicloud-cluster.k8s.local
spec:
  kubernetesVersion: v1.22.0
  cloudProvider: aws
  networking:
    calico:
      crossSubnet: true
  subnets:
  - name: aws-subnet
    type: Private
    zone: us-west-2a
    id: subnet-xxxxxxxx
  - name: gcp-subnet
    type: Private
    zone: us-central1-a
    id: subnet-yyyyyyyy
  api:
    loadBalancer:
      type: Internal
  additionalNetworkCIDRs:
  - 10.128.0.0/9
  - 10.0.0.0/8
```

Replace the subnet-xxxxxxxx and subnet-yyyyyyyy placeholders with your AWS and GCP subnet IDs, respectively.

Create the Kubernetes Cluster

Save the YAML file as multicloud-cluster.yaml. Then, use Kops to create the cluster:

```
kops create -f multicloud-cluster.yaml
kops create secret --name my-multicloud-cluster.k8s.local sshpublickey admin -
i ~/.ssh/id_rsa.pub
kops update cluster my-multicloud-cluster.k8s.local --yes
```

This process will take some time, as Kops will provision the necessary resources on both AWS and GCP.

Validate the Cluster

Once the process is complete, you can validate that your cluster is up and running:

```
kops validate cluster --name my-multicloud-cluster.k8s.local
```

Configure kubectl to Use New Cluster

To start using your new Kubernetes cluster, you'll need to configure kubectl:

```
kops export kubecfg --name my-multicloud-cluster.k8s.local
```

Test the Cluster

You can now deploy a sample application to ensure everything is working correctly:

```
kubectl create deployment hello-world --image=gcr.io/google-samples/node-
hello:1.0
kubectl expose deployment hello-world --type=LoadBalancer --port=8080 --
target-port=8080
```

After a few minutes, you should see an external IP address for the hello-world service:

```
kubectl get service hello world
```

Note the EXTERNAL-IP in the output:

```
NAME TYPE CLUSTER-IP EXTERNAL-IP PORT(S) AGE
hello-world LoadBalancer 10.100.200.123 123.45.67.89 8080:32123/TCP 3m
```

Access the Sample Application

Open a browser and navigate to the external IP address at port 8080: `http://123.45.67.89:8080` (replace `123.45.67.89` with your service's external IP address). You should see a "Hello, World!" message.

Clean Up Resources

To avoid incurring unnecessary costs, delete the resources when you're done experimenting with the cluster:

```
kubectl delete service hello-world
kubectl delete deployment hello-world
```

Wait for the LoadBalancer to be deleted before proceeding with the next step. To delete the cluster and all its associated resources, run:

```
kops delete cluster my-multicloud-cluster.k8s.local --yes
```

At this point, you should have enough experience in deploying a Kubernetes cluster that extends across various cloud providers using kubeadm and Kops. The cluster's specification can be tailored to your specific needs, such as incorporating additional nodes or utilizing distinct networking plugins. For further details on advanced configuration possibilities, refer to the official Kops documentation.

Deploying Applications on Kubernetes

Now that you have a multi-cloud Kubernetes cluster up and running, let's go through the process of deploying an application on it. In this section, we will walkthrough the steps to deploy an application on a multi-cloud Kubernetes cluster. First and foremost, you need to ensure that your cluster is up and running. Once you have verified this, we will proceed with the deployment process. For this sample demonstration, we will use a sample Node.js application.

Deploying an application on a Kubernetes cluster can be a complex process, but with the right guidance, it can be simplified. In our case, we will use Kubernetes to manage and orchestrate our application. Kubernetes provides a platform for deploying, scaling, and managing containerized applications. With Kubernetes, you can easily manage your application's lifecycle, from deployment to scaling and maintenance. We will start by building a Docker image of our Node.js application and then create a deployment using Kubernetes. Once our deployment is up and running, we can expose our application to the internet by creating a service. Finally, we will test our application to ensure that it is working as expected. By following these steps, you will have a solid understanding of how to deploy an application on a multi-cloud Kubernetes cluster.

Following is the step-by-step walkthrough to deploy applications::

Clone the Sample Application

Clone the sample Node.js application from the following repository:

```
git clone https://github.com/kubernetes/examples.git
cd examples/staging/nodejs/
```

Create Dockerfile

In the nodejs directory, create a Dockerfile with the following content:

```
FROM node:14

WORKDIR /app

COPY package*.json ./

RUN npm ci

COPY . .

EXPOSE 8080
```

```
CMD ["npm", "start"]
```

Build the Docker Image

Build the Docker image for the sample application:

```
docker build -t my-nodejs-app:1.0 .
```

Push Docker Image to Container Registry

You will need to push the Docker image to a container registry accessible by both AWS and GCP. For this sample demonstration, we'll use Docker Hub.

First, log in to Docker Hub:

```
docker login
```

Tag the image with your Docker Hub username:

```
docker tag my-nodejs-app:1.0 <your-dockerhub-username>/my-nodejs-app:1.0
```

Replace <your-dockerhub-username> with your actual Docker Hub username.

Now, push the image to Docker Hub:

```
docker push <your-dockerhub-username>/my-nodejs-app:1.0
```

Create Deployment YAML File

Create a new file called my-nodejs-app-deployment.yaml with the following content:

```
apiVersion: apps/v1
kind: Deployment
metadata:
  name: my-nodejs-app
spec:
```

```yaml
  replicas: 3
  selector:
   matchLabels:
    app: my-nodejs-app
  template:
   metadata:
    labels:
     app: my-nodejs-app
   spec:
    containers:
    - name: my-nodejs-app
      image: <your-dockerhub-username>/my-nodejs-app:1.0
      ports:
      - containerPort: 8080
---
apiVersion: v1
kind: Service
metadata:
 name: my-nodejs-app
spec:
 type: LoadBalancer
 ports:
 - port: 8080
   targetPort: 8080
   protocol: TCP
 selector:
  app: my-nodejs-app
```

Replace <your-dockerhub-username> with your actual Docker Hub username.

Deploy the Application

Deploy the application to your multi-cloud Kubernetes cluster:

```
kubectl apply -f my-nodejs-app-deployment.yaml
```

Monitor the Deployment

Check the status of the deployment:

```
kubectl rollout status deployment my-nodejs-app
```

Once the deployment is complete, you can check the created pods:

```
kubectl get pods -l app=my-nodejs-app
```

Access the Application

To access the application, you need to get the external IP address of the my-nodejs-app service:

```
kubectl get service my-nodejs-app
```

Note the EXTERNAL-IP in the output:

```
NAME            TYPE          CLUSTER-IP      EXTERNAL-IP      PORT(S)
AGE
my-nodejs-app  LoadBalancer   10.100.200.123   123.45.67.89
8080:32123/TCP   3m
```

Open a browser and navigate to the external IP address at port 8080: http://123.45.67.89:8080 (replace 123.45.67.89 with your service's external IP address). You should see the sample application running.

Scale the Application

If needed, you can scale the number of replicas for your application:

```
kubectl scale deployment my-nodejs-app --replicas=5
```

Check the updated number of pods:

```
kubectl get pods -l app=my-nodejs-app
```

Update the Application

To update the application, make changes to the source code, build a new Docker image with a different tag, push it to Docker Hub, and update the deployment. For example, update the image tag to 1.1:

```
# Build the new image
docker build -t my-nodejs-app:1.1 .

# Tag the image with your Docker Hub username
docker tag my-nodejs-app:1.1 <your-dockerhub-username>/my-nodejs-app:1.1

# Push the image to Docker Hub
docker push <your-dockerhub-username>/my-nodejs-app:1.1

# Update the deployment to use the new image
kubectl set image deployment my-nodejs-app my-nodejs-app=<your-dockerhub-username>/my-nodejs-app:1.1
```

Clean up Resources

To delete the resources associated with your application when you're done, run:

```
kubectl delete -f my-nodejs-app-deployment.yaml
```

This example demonstrated how to deploy, update, scale, and access a sample application on a multi-cloud Kubernetes cluster. By following these steps, you can deploy your own applications on your multi-cloud cluster.

Managing Deployments

Whether you're working with a multi-cloud Kubernetes cluster or a single-cloud one, managing deployments remains largely the same. In both cases, you'll rely on the same tool, kubectl, to interact with your deployments. This means that you won't need to worry about adjusting your approach depending on which cloud provider you're working with. Simply put, once you've mastered managing deployments in a single-cloud cluster, you'll be able to apply those same skills to a multi-cloud environment without too much difficulty.

Below are some common tasks to manage deployments on a multi-cloud Kubernetes cluster:

Get the List of Deployments

To see the list of deployments in your cluster, run:

```
kubectl get deployments
```

Get Detailed Information of Deployment

To see detailed information about a specific deployment, run:

```
kubectl describe deployment <deployment-name>
```

Replace <deployment-name> with the name of your deployment.

Update Number of Replicas

To scale a deployment, change the number of replicas:

```
kubectl scale deployment <deployment-name> --replicas=<number-of-replicas>
```

Replace <deployment-name> with the name of your deployment and <number-of-replicas> with the desired number of replicas.

Pause and Resume Deployment

You can pause a deployment to apply multiple changes and then resume it:

```
# Pause the deployment
kubectl rollout pause deployment <deployment-name>
```

```
# Apply multiple changes
kubectl set env deployment <deployment-name> KEY1=VALUE1
KEY2=VALUE2
kubectl set resources deployment <deployment-name> -c=<container-name> --
limits=cpu=200m,memory=512Mi


# Resume the deployment
kubectl rollout resume deployment <deployment-name>
```

Replace <deployment-name> and <container-name> with the names of your deployment and container, respectively.

Check the Rollout Status

Monitor the status of a rollout:

```
kubectl rollout status deployment <deployment-name>
```

Replace <deployment-name> with the name of your deployment.

View Rollout History

To view the rollout history of a deployment, run:

```
kubectl rollout history deployment <deployment-name>
```

Replace <deployment-name> with the name of your deployment.

These are some of the common tasks for managing deployments in a multi-cloud Kubernetes cluster. The kubectl command provides many other options to manage deployments, such as applying labels and annotations, updating configurations, and setting resource limits. You can find more information on managing deployments in the official Kubernetes documentation.

Rolling Updates

Kubernetes offers an important functionality called rolling updates which enables application updating with minimal interruption. Essentially, rolling updates work by gradually substituting older instances of the application with new ones in Kubernetes, ensuring that a certain number of replicas are always accessible. This way, even as the new version of the application is being deployed, users can continue to access a portion of the older version without any disruption to their experience.

Rolling updates are a critical aspect of managing and updating containerized applications, and Kubernetes provides a robust and reliable method for doing so. By minimizing downtime and allowing for a more seamless deployment process, rolling updates help ensure that applications remain up-to-date and functioning as intended while still providing users with uninterrupted access. With Kubernetes, developers have access to a range of powerful tools that allow them to easily and effectively manage and update containerized applications.

Below is how you can manage rolling updates for your deployments in a multi-cloud Kubernetes cluster:

Perform Rolling Update

To perform a rolling update for a specific deployment, you need to update the container image:

```
kubectl set image deployment <deployment-name> <container-name>=<new-image>
```

Replace <deployment-name> with the name of your deployment, <container-name> with the name of the container to update, and <new-image> with the new image.

For example, if you have a deployment named my-nodejs-app with a container named my-nodejs-app and you want to update the image to version 1.1, run:

```
kubectl set image deployment my-nodejs-app my-nodejs-app=<your-dockerhub-username>/my-nodejs-app:1.1
```

Kubernetes will gradually replace the old instances with new ones, ensuring that the application remains available throughout the update process.

Monitor Rollout Status

You can check the status of the rollout using the following command:

```
kubectl rollout status deployment <deployment-name>
```

Replace <deployment-name> with the name of your deployment.

Pause and Resume Rollout

You can pause a rollout to apply multiple changes at once or to debug issues, and then resume it later:

```
# Pause the rollout
kubectl rollout pause deployment <deployment-name>

# Make changes or debug issues
# ...

# Resume the rollout
kubectl rollout resume deployment <deployment-name>
```

Replace <deployment-name> with the name of your deployment.

Rollback to Previous Version

If you encounter issues after a rolling update, you can roll back to a previous version of the deployment:

```
kubectl rollout undo deployment <deployment-name>
```

Replace <deployment-name> with the name of your deployment.

View Rollout History

To view the rollout history of a deployment, run:

```
kubectl rollout history deployment <deployment-name>
```

Replace <deployment-name> with the name of your deployment.

Rollback to Specific Revision

If you want to roll back to a specific revision, use the --to-revision flag:

```
kubectl rollout undo deployment <deployment-name> --to-revision=<revision-number>
```

Replace <deployment-name> with the name of your deployment and <revision-number> with the desired revision number.

By using these commands and techniques, you can effectively manage rolling updates for your deployments in a multi-cloud Kubernetes cluster, ensuring minimal downtime and a smoother update process.

Scaling and Autoscaling

Kubernetes offers a scalable infrastructure for managing containerized applications by providing the ability to adjust the number of replicas of a deployment to meet the demands of varying workloads. This process of adjusting the number of replicas is known as scaling. In Kubernetes, scaling can be done manually or automatically. Automatic scaling is referred to as autoscaling, and it involves adjusting the number of replicas based on workload metrics, such as CPU utilization.

Autoscaling is an essential feature in Kubernetes because it helps to optimize resource utilization while maintaining application performance. When the workload increases, autoscaling ensures that the application can handle the increased load by scaling up the number of replicas. Conversely, when the workload decreases, autoscaling reduces the number of replicas to avoid resource wastage. This automated process saves time and effort compared to manual scaling, and it ensures that the application is always running optimally.

Below is how you can manage scaling and autoscaling in a multi-cloud Kubernetes cluster:

Manual Scaling

Scale a deployment:
To manually scale a deployment, change the number of replicas using the kubectl scale command:

```
kubectl scale deployment <deployment-name> --replicas=<number-of-
```

replicas>

Replace <deployment-name> with the name of your deployment and <number-of-replicas> with the desired number of replicas.

Verify the scaling

Check the updated number of pods:

```
kubectl get pods -l app=<deployment-name>
```

Replace <deployment-name> with the name of your deployment.

Autoscaling

To enable autoscaling, you need to use the Kubernetes Horizontal Pod Autoscaler (HPA). The HPA adjusts the number of replicas based on the observed CPU utilization or other custom metrics.

Create an HPA resource

To create an HPA resource, use the kubectl autoscale command:

```
kubectl autoscale deployment <deployment-name> --min=<min-replicas> --max=<max-replicas> --cpu-percent=<target-cpu-utilization>
```

Replace <deployment-name> with the name of your deployment, <min-replicas> with the minimum number of replicas, <max-replicas> with the maximum number of replicas, and <target-cpu-utilization> with the desired target CPU utilization percentage.

For example, to create an HPA for a deployment named my-nodejs-app with a minimum of 3 replicas, a maximum of 10 replicas, and a target CPU utilization of 50%, run:

```
kubectl autoscale deployment my-nodejs-app --min=3 --max=10 --cpu-percent=50
```

Verify the HPA

Check the created HPA resource:

```
kubectl get hpa
```

You should see the HPA resource with the target CPU utilization and the current number of replicas.

Monitor the HPA

To see detailed information about the HPA, run:

```
kubectl describe hpa <hpa-name>
```

Replace <hpa-name> with the name of your HPA resource, which is usually the same as the deployment name.

Update the HPA

To update the HPA configuration, such as changing the target CPU utilization or the minimum/maximum number of replicas, use the kubectl edit command:

```
kubectl edit hpa <hpa-name>
```

Replace <hpa-name> with the name of your HPA resource.
This will open the HPA resource configuration in your default text editor. Make the necessary changes and save the file.

Delete the HPA

To remove the HPA and disable autoscaling, run:

```
kubectl delete hpa <hpa-name>
```

Replace <hpa-name> with the name of your HPA resource.

By following these steps, you can effectively scale and autoscale your deployments in a multi-cloud Kubernetes cluster, ensuring that your applications can handle varying workloads and maintain optimal performance.

Explore Helm Package Manager

Helm is a package manager for Kubernetes that simplifies the deployment, management, and scaling of applications on Kubernetes clusters. It streamlines the process of defining, installing, and upgrading Kubernetes resources by using a packaging format called "charts." A chart is a collection of files that describe a related set of Kubernetes resources.

In a multi-cloud Kubernetes environment, applications and services often need to be deployed and managed across different cloud providers, such as AWS, Azure, GCP, or on-premises data centers. This adds complexity to the application management process, as each cloud provider has its own set of tools, APIs, and configurations.

Helm plays a critical role in multi-cloud Kubernetes environments by providing a consistent way to manage applications across different cloud providers. It offers several advantages:

- Simplified deployment: Helm charts encapsulate the complexity of deploying applications on Kubernetes, allowing you to deploy a pre-configured application with a single command.
- Consistency: Helm ensures that deployments are consistent across different cloud providers by abstracting away the differences in APIs, tooling, and configurations. This means you can use the same Helm chart to deploy your application on any Kubernetes cluster, regardless of the cloud provider.
- Versioning and rollback: Helm allows you to version your application deployments, making it easy to upgrade or rollback to a previous version if needed.
- Reusability and sharing: Helm charts can be easily shared and reused, enabling you to leverage pre-built configurations and best practices from the community.
- Customization: Helm charts are highly customizable, allowing you to configure application deployments to suit your specific needs.
- Ecosystem integration: Helm integrates with other tools in the Kubernetes ecosystem, such as continuous integration and continuous deployment (CI/CD) pipelines, monitoring tools, and security solutions, facilitating seamless deployment and management.

In summary, Helm is an essential tool for managing applications in a multi-cloud Kubernetes environment. It simplifies deployment and management, provides consistency across different cloud providers, and offers a range of other benefits that make it an integral part of the Kubernetes ecosystem.

Install and Configure Helm

Deploying applications in a multi-cloud Kubernetes environment can be a complex task, but it can be made easier by using the right tools and following the right steps. One such tool is Helm, a popular package manager for Kubernetes that streamlines the deployment and management of applications. In this section, we will go through the steps you need to take to install and set up Helm in a multi-cloud Kubernetes environment.

Install Helm CLI

The first step in using Helm is to install the Helm CLI on your local machine. You can do this by visiting the official Helm GitHub repository and downloading the appropriate version for your operating system. Once you have downloaded the Helm CLI, follow the installation instructions provided in the README file.

Set up Kubernetes Clusters

To use Helm in a multi-cloud Kubernetes environment, you need to have access to multiple Kubernetes clusters running on different cloud providers. Ensure that you have the required credentials, such as kubeconfig files or API keys, to access and manage these clusters. You can use tools like kubectl to verify your access to the clusters.

Configure Context

Once you have access to the Kubernetes clusters, ensure that your local Kubernetes configuration has the contexts set up for each cluster in the multi-cloud environment. This is usually stored in ~/.kube/config. You can use kubectl config use-context <context-name> to switch between different clusters.

Install and Configure Cloud Provider-specific Components

Some cloud providers may require additional components or configurations for their specific storage, networking, or other services. Ensure that these components are installed and configured correctly in your Kubernetes clusters. This may include configuring the cloud provider's Container Network Interface (CNI), ingress controllers, storage classes, etc.

Create Helm Charts

To deploy your applications using Helm, you will need Helm charts. You can either create your own charts from scratch or customize existing charts from community repositories like the Helm Hub. Make sure to test your charts for compatibility across different cloud providers.

Set up Continuous Integration and Continuous Deployment

Configure a CI/CD pipeline to automate the deployment and management of your applications across the multi-cloud Kubernetes environment. This can involve tools like Jenkins, GitLab CI/CD, or GitHub Actions. Ensure that your pipeline deploys the applications to the appropriate Kubernetes clusters using Helm.

Monitoring and Logging

Set up monitoring and logging solutions that can collect and aggregate data from your multi-cloud Kubernetes environment. Tools like Prometheus for monitoring and Elasticsearch, Fluentd, and Kibana (EFK) for logging can help you gain insights into your applications' performance across different cloud providers.

Security

Ensure that your multi-cloud Kubernetes environment adheres to best security practices, such as network segmentation, role-based access control (RBAC), and encryption for data at rest and in transit.

By following these steps, you can have Helm ready for use in your multi-cloud Kubernetes environment. With Helm, you can deploy and manage applications consistently across different cloud providers, leveraging its features to streamline and optimize your deployment process. By setting up monitoring and logging solutions and adhering to best security practices, you can ensure that your applications are running smoothly and securely.

Ingress Controllers and Load Balancing

Kubernetes is a popular container orchestration platform that requires efficient traffic management for optimal performance. To this end, two crucial components are used:
- Ingress Controllers, and
- Load Balancing

Ingress Controllers serve as the entry point for incoming traffic to your applications and manage the routing of requests to their respective services. Load Balancing ensures that the traffic is distributed evenly among the available services, thereby preventing any one service from being overwhelmed by too much traffic. These two components are essential for the efficient management of incoming traffic to your applications and ensuring their smooth operation in a Kubernetes environment.

Ingress Controllers

An Ingress Controller is a Kubernetes component that watches the API server for Ingress resources and processes the rules defined in those resources. It is responsible for managing external access to the services running in a cluster, usually by enabling HTTP and HTTPS routing.

In a multi-cloud Kubernetes environment, Ingress Controllers help to provide a consistent interface for managing external access to your applications across different cloud providers. This consistency allows you to define routing rules once, and the Ingress Controller will adapt those rules for the specific cloud provider.

There are several Ingress Controllers available, each with its own set of features and configurations. Some popular Ingress Controllers include:
- NGINX Ingress Controller: A widely-used Ingress Controller based on the NGINX web server and reverse proxy. It offers robust features, high performance, and a large community.
- HAProxy Ingress Controller: Based on the HAProxy load balancer, this Ingress Controller is known for its high performance and reliability. It is suitable for large-scale deployments with high traffic.
- Traefik: A modern, dynamic, and feature-rich Ingress Controller and reverse proxy. Traefik is designed to be easy to configure and supports automatic discovery of services, making it suitable for microservices and containerized environments.
- AWS ALB Ingress Controller: A Kubernetes-native Ingress Controller for AWS Application Load Balancer (ALB). It allows you to leverage AWS-specific features and integrate with other AWS services like WAF and Shield.
- GKE Ingress Controller: This Ingress Controller is built-in and managed by Google Kubernetes Engine (GKE). It uses Google Cloud Load Balancer to manage external access to your services.

Load Balancing

Load balancing is the process of distributing network traffic across multiple servers to ensure that no single server is overwhelmed. In Kubernetes, load balancing can be implemented at different levels:
- Service level: Kubernetes provides built-in support for load balancing using the Service resource with a type of LoadBalancer. The cloud provider provisions a cloud-specific load balancer that distributes traffic among the Pods backing the Service.
- Ingress level: Ingress Controllers often integrate with cloud provider-specific load balancers, distributing traffic to the backend services based on the Ingress rules.

- Load balancing solutions for multi-cloud environments can vary depending on the cloud provider and Ingress Controller. Some available options include:
- Cloud provider-specific load balancers: Each cloud provider offers its load balancer solution, such as AWS ELB/ALB, Google Cloud Load Balancer, and Azure Load Balancer. These load balancers can be used with the respective cloud provider's Ingress Controller.
- Cross-cloud load balancing solutions: Some third-party load balancing solutions can be used across multiple cloud providers. For example, F5 BIG-IP, Avi Networks (VMware NSX Advanced Load Balancer), and Citrix ADC provide multi-cloud load balancing capabilities.

By using Ingress Controllers and Load Balancing in a multi-cloud Kubernetes environment, you can ensure consistent management of incoming traffic and efficient distribution of requests across your services, regardless of the cloud provider. This results in improved performance, reliability, and scalability for your applications.

Monitoring and Logging

Monitoring and logging for multi-cloud Kubernetes environments are essential to ensure the performance, reliability, and security of your applications. These practices help you identify issues, diagnose problems, and optimize resource usage across different cloud providers.

Monitoring in multi-cloud Kubernetes involves collecting metrics and performance data from your clusters, nodes, and applications. This data helps you to:
- Understand the health and performance of your clusters and applications.
- Identify performance bottlenecks, resource constraints, and other issues.
- Detect and resolve security and compliance issues.
- Make informed decisions about scaling and optimizing your infrastructure.

Logging, on the other hand, focuses on collecting and analyzing logs generated by your clusters, nodes, applications, and other Kubernetes components. Logging helps you to:
- Debug and troubleshoot application issues and errors.
- Monitor user activities and detect security incidents.
- Comply with regulatory and audit requirements.
- Gain insights into application and infrastructure behavior for optimization.

There are several open-source tools available for monitoring and logging in multi-cloud Kubernetes environments. Some of the best and most popular include:
- Prometheus: A widely used monitoring system that collects and stores time-series metrics from your Kubernetes clusters. It integrates with Kubernetes using custom

resource definitions and supports querying, alerting, and dashboarding using Grafana.

- Grafana: A popular visualization and analytics platform that can integrate with Prometheus and other data sources to create customizable, interactive dashboards for monitoring your Kubernetes clusters and applications.
- Fluentd: A flexible and extensible log collection and forwarding system that can aggregate logs from various sources in your Kubernetes clusters and forward them to different storage and analysis systems. It can be used with Elasticsearch and Kibana to create a comprehensive logging solution.
- Elasticsearch and Kibana: Elasticsearch is a powerful search and analytics engine, and Kibana is a visualization tool that works with Elasticsearch. Together, they form the popular ELK Stack (Elasticsearch, Logstash, and Kibana) used for log aggregation, storage, and analysis.
- Jaeger: A distributed tracing system that helps you monitor and troubleshoot transactions in complex, distributed systems like microservices running on Kubernetes. It provides end-to-end latency tracking, dependency analysis, and performance optimization.

These tools can be used individually or in combination to create a comprehensive monitoring and logging solution for your multi-cloud Kubernetes environments.

Summary

We discussed the process of setting up a Kubernetes cluster and deploying applications on multi-cloud Kubernetes. The steps involved include configuring AWS and GCP credentials for multi-cloud use, configuring kubectl to use the new cluster, testing the cluster, and managing deployments.

To set up a Kubernetes cluster, one needs to configure the necessary infrastructure in their preferred cloud provider. This includes creating the required virtual machines, installing and configuring Kubernetes, and setting up the necessary networking components. Once this is done, one can then configure AWS and GCP credentials for multi-cloud use to ensure that Kubernetes can access resources in both cloud providers. Next, one needs to configure kubectl to use the new cluster. This involves creating a kubeconfig file that specifies the necessary cluster information, authentication details, and context information. With kubectl properly configured, one can then test the cluster by deploying a sample application and verifying that it is running correctly.

Deploying applications on multi-cloud Kubernetes involves creating deployment YAML files that specify the necessary containers, replicas, and other configuration options. Once the deployment is created, one can manage it using kubectl commands such as scaling up or down, rolling updates, and manual scaling. To ensure that the Kubernetes cluster is highly available and can handle increased traffic, one can explore Helm, Ingress controllers, and load balancing. Helm is a package manager for Kubernetes that allows one to easily deploy and manage applications. Ingress controllers provide a way to route external traffic to internal services running on the cluster, while load balancing ensures that traffic is distributed evenly across the cluster.

Finally, it is important to note that Kubernetes also supports autoscaling, which allows the cluster to automatically adjust the number of replicas based on the workload. This ensures that the cluster is always optimized for performance while minimizing costs.

CHAPTER 3: USING FluxCD

Overview of FluxCD

Importance of Continuous Delivery for Multicloud Kubernetes

Continuous Delivery (CD) is a software development practice that enables teams to release software changes rapidly, reliably, and automatically. In the context of multicloud Kubernetes, CD becomes particularly important for several reasons:

- Consistency: Multicloud Kubernetes environments involve multiple cloud providers and on-premises infrastructure. CD ensures that application releases are consistent across all environments, reducing the risk of inconsistencies and unexpected behaviors.
- Speed and Agility: CD enables development teams to push changes to production faster, reducing the time it takes to deliver new features, fix bugs, and respond to customer needs. This allows organizations to stay competitive and keep up with the fast pace of the software industry.
- Automation: CD automates the deployment process, minimizing human intervention and reducing the chance of errors. This leads to more reliable and stable deployments, allowing teams to focus on higher-value tasks.
- Scalability: As the number of services and deployments increases in a multicloud Kubernetes environment, manual deployment processes become unsustainable. CD supports scalable deployment processes, ensuring that new services can be added seamlessly.
- Enhanced Collaboration: CD encourages collaboration between development and operations teams by integrating their workflows. This enables better communication and faster resolution of issues, leading to improved overall software quality.

Evolution of FluxCD as Continuous Delivery Tool

FluxCD is a popular open-source continuous delivery tool specifically designed for Kubernetes. It has evolved over time to address the unique challenges associated with managing deployments in multicloud environments:

- Flux v1: Flux v1, the first iteration of FluxCD, provided a GitOps-based approach for managing Kubernetes resources. It allowed teams to define their desired state in a Git repository, and Flux would automatically synchronize the cluster state with the repository. This ensured that the actual state always matched the desired state.
- Helm Operator: In response to the growing popularity of Helm, a Kubernetes package manager, Flux introduced the Helm Operator. This addition allowed users to manage Helm releases directly from Git repositories, further simplifying the deployment process.

- Flux v2: Flux v2 was a complete rewrite of the project, introducing several improvements over Flux v1, such as a more modular architecture, support for custom resources, improved performance, and better observability. Flux v2 also introduced support for multi-tenancy and other advanced GitOps features, making it more suitable for large-scale and multicloud deployments.
- Flux and Flagger: Flagger is a progressive delivery tool that integrates with FluxCD to provide advanced deployment strategies such as canary releases, A/B testing, and blue-green deployments. The integration of Flagger into the Flux ecosystem enables teams to deploy applications more safely, reducing the risk of downtime and negative user experiences.

As FluxCD continues to evolve, it is likely to incorporate new features and integrations that further enhance its capabilities as a continuous delivery tool for multicloud Kubernetes environments.

GitOps Principles and Workflow

GitOps is a set of practices that combines Git, the popular version control system, with infrastructure as code (IaC) principles and continuous delivery (CD) to manage and deploy applications and infrastructure. The term "GitOps" was coined by Weaveworks, and it aims to improve automation, traceability, and consistency across the entire software development and deployment process.

Below is an in-depth look at GitOps principles and workflows in about 1000 words:

GitOps Principles

Declarative Configuration

GitOps relies on declarative configuration management, where the desired state of the system is defined in a human-readable format (such as YAML or JSON). This enables teams to express their infrastructure and application configurations in a clear, concise manner that is easy to understand and version.

Version Control

GitOps leverages Git as the single source of truth for managing the desired state of the system. All changes to the system are made through Git, ensuring that there's a clear audit trail, and enabling teams to track, review, and roll back changes as needed.

Automated Convergence

GitOps uses automation to converge the actual state of the system with the desired state defined in Git. This is typically achieved using operators or controllers that watch for changes in the Git repository and automatically apply those changes to the system. This eliminates manual intervention and reduces the risk of human error.

Observability and Verification

In GitOps, the actual state of the system is continuously observed and compared to the desired state defined in Git. Any discrepancies between the two are flagged, and corrective actions are taken to bring the system back to the desired state. This ensures that the system remains consistent and stable at all times.

GitOps Workflows

Defining the Desired State

The first step in a GitOps workflow is to define the desired state of the system using declarative configuration files. These files typically include Kubernetes manifests, Helm charts, or other infrastructure as code (IaC) tools like Terraform or CloudFormation templates. The configuration files are stored in a Git repository, which serves as the single source of truth for the system's desired state.

Implementing Changes

When changes to the system are required, such as deploying a new application version or modifying infrastructure settings, developers make the necessary updates to the configuration files in their local Git working copies. They then commit and push these changes to the remote Git repository.

Pull Requests and Code Review

Before changes are merged into the main branch, a pull request is created to enable peer review and ensure that the proposed changes meet the team's quality standards. This step helps catch potential issues early in the process and fosters collaboration between team members.

Merging and Continuous Integration (CI)

Once the changes are approved, they are merged into the main branch. At this point, continuous integration (CI) pipelines are triggered to build, test, and validate the updated configuration files. This helps ensure that the changes do not introduce any bugs, security vulnerabilities, or other issues that could negatively impact the system.

Continuous Delivery (CD) and Convergence

After the changes pass the CI checks, the continuous delivery (CD) process begins. In a

GitOps workflow, this typically involves a Kubernetes operator or controller that monitors the Git repository for changes. When it detects updates to the main branch, it automatically applies the changes to the system, ensuring that the actual state converges with the desired state defined in Git. This step may also involve additional verification, such as monitoring the health of the deployed application or infrastructure components.

Monitoring and Observability

With the changes deployed, the system's actual state is continuously monitored and compared to the desired state in Git. GitOps tools often include built-in observability features, such as logging, metrics, and tracing, to provide insights into the system's performance and behavior. If any discrepancies between the actual and desired states are detected, the GitOps tool alerts the team and may automatically initiate corrective actions to bring the system back in line with the desired state.

Rollbacks and Recovery

One of the key benefits of GitOps is the ability to easily roll back changes in case of issues or failures. Since all changes are versioned in Git, rolling back to a previous state is as simple as reverting to an earlier commit and allowing the GitOps tool to automatically converge the system to that state. This helps minimize downtime and ensures rapid recovery from incidents.

Security and Compliance

GitOps workflows enable better security and compliance by providing a clear audit trail of all changes made to the system. This makes it easier to track who made changes, when they were made, and why they were made. Additionally, GitOps tools often integrate with existing security and compliance tools, such as policy engines or vulnerability scanners, to ensure that the deployed configurations meet the organization's security and compliance requirements.

Scaling and Multi-tenancy

GitOps is designed to scale with the complexity of modern cloud-native applications and infrastructure. As the number of services, environments, and teams grows, GitOps workflows can be adapted to support multi-tenancy and ensure that each team can manage its own configurations independently while maintaining a consistent and unified approach to managing the system's desired state.

In summary, GitOps is a powerful approach to managing and deploying applications and infrastructure in a cloud-native world. By leveraging declarative configurations, Git as the single source of truth, and automation to converge the system's actual state with its desired state, GitOps workflows provide greater consistency, traceability, and reliability. These practices help teams deliver high-quality software faster, minimize downtime, and ensure that their systems remain secure and compliant at all times.

Installing and Configuring FluxCD

Installing and configuring FluxCD for multicloud Kubernetes involves several steps. Below is a step-by-step walkthrough to help you set up FluxCD in a multicloud environment:

Install Flux CLI

The first step is to install the Flux command-line interface (CLI) on your local machine. You can download the latest version of the CLI from the FluxCD GitHub repository. To install the Flux CLI, follow the instructions for your operating system at
https://fluxcd.io/install/

Set Up Git Repositories

FluxCD uses Git repositories to store your Kubernetes manifests, Helm charts, or other infrastructure configuration files. For multicloud Kubernetes, you may choose to have separate Git repositories for each cloud provider or organize your manifests using directories within a single repository.

Create a Git repository for each cluster or environment, and push your configuration files to these repositories. Make sure you have access to these repositories from your local machine, as you'll need to provide the repository URLs during the FluxCD setup process.

Authenticate with Kubernetes Clusters

To deploy FluxCD to your multicloud Kubernetes clusters, you'll need to authenticate with each cluster. Use the appropriate credentials and context for each cluster in your Kubernetes configuration file (usually located at ~/.kube/config). You can use kubectl config use-context to switch between cluster contexts.

Install FluxCD on Multicloud Kubernetes Clusters

With the Flux CLI installed and your repositories set up, you can now install FluxCD on each of your Kubernetes clusters. To do this, run the following command for each cluster, replacing <YOUR-GIT-REPOSITORY> with the URL of the corresponding Git repository:

```
flux bootstrap git --url <YOUR-GIT-REPOSITORY> --path=<PATH-TO-
```

CLUSTER-CONFIGURATION> [--token-auth] [--network-policy] [--private]
[--version=<VERSION>]

Make sure you switch to the appropriate context for each cluster before running this command. The --path flag is optional and is used to specify a subdirectory within the repository containing the cluster-specific configuration files. The other optional flags can be used for additional configuration, such as using a personal access token for authentication, setting up network policies, or specifying a specific Flux version.

Configure FluxCD for Multicloud Environments

Once FluxCD is installed on each cluster, you can configure it to synchronize the desired state from the corresponding Git repositories. To do this, create a Kustomization resource for each cluster. This resource tells FluxCD which Git repository and path to use for synchronization, as well as other settings, such as the synchronization interval.

Below is an example Kustomization resource:

```
apiVersion: kustomize.toolkit.fluxcd.io/v1beta2
kind: Kustomization
metadata:
  name: my-cluster
  namespace: flux-system
spec:
  interval: 1m
  path: ./path/to/cluster/configuration
  prune: true
  sourceRef:
    kind: GitRepository
    name: my-git-repository
  validation: client
```

Replace the path with the path to your cluster-specific configuration files within the Git repository. Create a similar Kustomization resource for each cluster and commit these files to your Git repositories.

Monitor and Manage Multicloud Deployments

With FluxCD installed and configured on your multicloud Kubernetes clusters, it will now automatically synchronize the desired state from the Git repositories to the clusters. You can use the Flux CLI to monitor the synchronization status and manage your deployments.

To check the status of your deployments, run:

flux get kustomizations

To manage your deployments, simply update the configuration files in the Git repositories and commit the changes to trigger a new synchronization with FluxCD. You can also use the Flux CLI to automate deployments, monitor health checks, and manage rollouts.

Below are a few additional tips and best practices for installing and configuring FluxCD in a multicloud environment:

- Use Git submodules or Git subdirectories to organize your configuration files within the Git repository. This can make it easier to manage large numbers of clusters or environments.
- Use Git branches to manage different versions of your configurations. For example, you can use a prod branch for your production environment and a dev branch for your development environment.
- Use Git tags to mark specific versions of your configuration files, such as a specific release or a critical hotfix.
- Use FluxCD's GitOps toolkit features to automate the management of your Kubernetes resources, such as creating namespaces, RBAC rules, or secrets.
- Use FluxCD's advanced features, such as canary releases or progressive delivery, to deploy new features or updates in a controlled and safe manner.
- Monitor your FluxCD installations and Git repositories using tools such as Prometheus, Grafana, or Kibana to gain insights into the health and performance of your deployments.

In summary, installing and configuring FluxCD for multicloud Kubernetes involves setting up Git repositories, authenticating with your Kubernetes clusters, and creating Kustomization resources to define the desired state of your system. With FluxCD in place, you can automate the synchronization of your configurations and manage your deployments using GitOps workflows. By following these best practices and using FluxCD's advanced features, you can ensure that your multicloud Kubernetes deployments are consistent, reliable, and scalable.

Continuous Delivery with FluxCD

FluxCD achieves CD by automating the various stages of the software delivery pipeline. When new code is merged into the main branch, FluxCD automatically detects the changes and triggers a deployment process. The new version of the application is then built, tested, and deployed to the production environment in a repeatable and predictable manner.

FluxCD also includes several advanced features such as canary releases, blue/green deployments, and rollbacks. These features allow teams to test new versions of their applications in a controlled manner before rolling them out to production. In the event of a problem, FluxCD can automatically roll back to a previous version of the application, ensuring that downtime is minimized and that the system remains highly available.

Below is a step-by-step walkthrough to perform continuous delivery with FluxCD:

Configure the Git Repository

In order to set up FluxCD for Kubernetes, you will need to configure a Git repository to act as the "single source of truth" for your cluster's desired state. This can be a new Git repository or an existing one that you will use to store your Kubernetes manifests and FluxCD configuration.

Connect FluxCD to Kubernetes Cluster

Once you have set up your Git repository, you will need to connect FluxCD to your Kubernetes cluster. To do this, run the following command, replacing the placeholders with your own information:

```
flux bootstrap <GIT_PROVIDER> --repository=<USERNAME>/<REPO_NAME> --path=<PATH_IN_REPO> --personal
```

The GIT_PROVIDER should be replaced with the name of the Git provider you're using (e.g., github, gitlab, bitbucket), USERNAME with your own username, REPO_NAME with the name of the repository you've created, and PATH_IN_REPO with the path in the repository where you'll store your FluxCD configuration. The --personal flag indicates that you're using a personal repository.

Create FluxCD Configuration

Once you have connected FluxCD to your Kubernetes cluster, you'll need to create a new folder in your Git repository to store your FluxCD configuration. Within this folder, add a kustomization.yaml file with the following content:

```yaml
apiVersion: kustomize.config.k8s.io/v1beta1
kind: Kustomization


resources:
- flux-system
```

This file will include the flux-system directory in the configuration.

Define Application's Kubernetes Manifests

Next, create another new folder in your Git repository to store your application's Kubernetes manifests. Add your application's Kubernetes YAML files, such as deployments, services, and ingress resources, to this folder.

Synchronize the Application's Manifests

To synchronize your application's manifests with FluxCD, add a new kustomization.yaml file to your application's folder with the following content:

```yaml
apiVersion: kustomize.config.k8s.io/v1beta1
kind: Kustomization


resources:
- <APP_MANIFEST_FILE_1>
- <APP_MANIFEST_FILE_2>

...
```

Replace <APP_MANIFEST_FILE_1>, <APP_MANIFEST_FILE_2>, etc., with the filenames of your application's Kubernetes manifests.

<u>Add Application to FluxCD Configuration</u>

In the kustomization.yaml file you created in step 4, add a reference to the application's folder:

```
apiVersion: kustomize.config.k8s.io/v1beta1
kind: Kustomization

resources:
- flux-system
- <APP_FOLDER>
```

Replace <APP_FOLDER> with the name of the folder containing your application's Kubernetes manifests.

Commit and Push Changes

Commit your changes to the Git repository and push them to the remote. FluxCD will detect the changes and apply them to the connected Kubernetes cluster.

Monitor Synchronization Status

Use the Flux CLI to monitor the synchronization status:

```
flux get kustomizations
```

This command will display the current status of your configured Kustomizations, showing if they are successfully synchronized with your cluster.

From this point on, any changes you push to the Git repository will be automatically detected and applied by FluxCD. You can also use the Flux CLI to perform actions such as pausing or resuming synchronization, or checking the status of resources in your cluster.

Managing Secrets and ConfigMaps

Managing Secrets and ConfigMaps with FluxCD is an essential part of handling sensitive data and configurations for your applications. Secrets store sensitive data, while ConfigMaps store non-sensitive configuration data. FluxCD can manage both of these resources using its Kustomize integration.

Below is a step-by-step walkthrough to managing Secrets and ConfigMaps with FluxCD:

Create New Folder for Application's Configuration

Create a new folder in your Git repository that will store your application's Secrets and ConfigMaps. For example, you can name this folder 'config'.

Create ConfigMap YAML File

Create a new file in the config folder called configmap.yaml with the following content:

```yaml
apiVersion: v1
kind: ConfigMap
metadata:
  name: my-configmap
data:
  my-key: my-value
  another-key: another-value
```

Replace my-configmap with the desired name for your ConfigMap, and add key-value pairs under data as needed for your application.

Create Secret YAML File

If you need to manage sensitive data, create a new file in the config folder called secret.yaml. Since storing sensitive data in plain text is not secure, you should encode the values using base64. You can use the following template:

```yaml
apiVersion: v1
kind: Secret
type: Opaque
metadata:
  name: my-secret
data:
  secret-key: c2VjcmV0LXZhbHVl
```

Replace my-secret with the desired name for your Secret, and add key-value pairs under data as needed. Make sure to encode the values in base64 format.

To encode a value in base64, you can use a command like the following:

```
echo -n 'your-secret-value' | base64
```

Create Kustomization File

In the config folder, create a new kustomization.yaml file with the following content:

```
apiVersion: kustomize.config.k8s.io/v1beta1
kind: Kustomization

resources:
- configmap.yaml
- secret.yaml
```

Remove the - secret.yaml line if you don't have any Secrets to manage.

Update Main Kustomization File

In the kustomization.yaml file you created in the previous steps, add a reference to the config folder:

```
apiVersion: kustomize.config.k8s.io/v1beta1
kind: Kustomization

resources:
- flux-system
- <APP_FOLDER>
- config
```

Replace <APP_FOLDER> with the name of the folder containing your application's Kubernetes manifests.

Commit and Push Changes

Commit the changes to the Git repository and push them to the remote. FluxCD will detect the changes and apply the ConfigMaps and Secrets to the connected Kubernetes cluster.

Use ConfigMaps and Secrets in Application

In your application's Kubernetes manifests, you can now reference the created ConfigMaps and Secrets. For example, in a Deployment manifest, you can mount a ConfigMap or Secret as a volume or use them as environment variables:

```
apiVersion: apps/v1
kind: Deployment
metadata:
  name: my-deployment
spec:
  template:
    spec:
      containers:
      - name: my-container
        image: my-image
        env:
        - name: MY_CONFIG_KEY
          valueFrom:
            configMapKeyRef:
              name: my-configmap
              key: my-key
        - name: MY_SECRET_KEY
          valueFrom:
            secret
KeyRef:
name: my-secret
key: secret-key
volumeMounts:
- name: config-volume
```

mountPath: /etc/config
- name: secret-volume
mountPath: /etc/secret
volumes:
- name: config-volume
configMap:
name: my-configmap
- name: secret-volume
secret:
secretName: my-secret

In the above demonstrated example, the Deployment manifest mounts the ConfigMap as a volume at `/etc/config` and the Secret as a volume at `/etc/secret`. Additionally, it sets the environment variables `MY_CONFIG_KEY` and `MY_SECRET_KEY` using the values from the ConfigMap and Secret, respectively.

By following these steps, you can effectively manage Secrets and ConfigMaps with FluxCD. Any changes you make to your ConfigMaps and Secrets in your Git repository will be automatically detected and applied by FluxCD. This approach ensures that your sensitive data and application configurations are version-controlled, secure, and easily managed.

Monitoring and Alerting with FluxCD

Monitoring and alerting are essential aspects of managing a Kubernetes cluster with FluxCD. By setting up monitoring and alerting, you can gain insights into the health and performance of your cluster, as well as be notified of any issues. FluxCD emits Prometheus metrics, which can be used to monitor the system, and you can use alerting tools like Alertmanager to send notifications based on these metrics.

Below is a step-by-step walkthrough to set up monitoring and alerting with FluxCD:

Install Prometheus and Alertmanager

If you don't have Prometheus and Alertmanager installed in your cluster, you can use the kube-prometheus-stack Helm chart to set them up.

Configure Prometheus to Scrape FluxCD Metrics

FluxCD components (source-controller, kustomize-controller, helm-controller, and notification-controller) expose metrics on the /metrics endpoint. You'll need to create a ServiceMonitor resource to tell Prometheus to scrape metrics from these components. Create a file called service-monitor.yaml with the following content:

```yaml
apiVersion: monitoring.coreos.com/v1
kind: ServiceMonitor
metadata:
  name: fluxcd
  namespace: flux-system
  labels:
    release: prometheus
spec:
  selector:
    matchLabels:
      app.kubernetes.io/part-of: flux
  namespaceSelector:
    matchNames:
    - flux-system
  endpoints:
  - port: http-metrics
    interval: 30s
```

This configuration tells Prometheus to scrape metrics from services in the flux-system namespace with the label app.kubernetes.io/part-of: flux. Adjust the labels and namespace if you have a custom setup.

Apply ServiceMonitor Resource

Apply the service-monitor.yaml file to your Kubernetes cluster:

```
kubectl apply -f service-monitor.yaml
```

Set up Custom Alerts

You can create custom alerts based on FluxCD metrics using Prometheus Alertmanager. First, create a new file called flux-alerts.yaml with the following content:

```yaml
apiVersion: monitoring.coreos.com/v1
kind: PrometheusRule
metadata:
  name: fluxcd-alerts
  namespace: flux-system
spec:
  groups:
  - name: FluxCD
    rules:
    - alert: FluxCDReconciliationFailure
      expr: rate(flux_reconcile_failure_count{namespace="flux-system"}[5m]) > 0
      for: 10m
      labels:
        severity: warning
      annotations:
        summary: "FluxCD reconciliation failure"
        description: "FluxCD has been failing to reconcile resources for the last 10 minutes."
```

This example creates an alert called FluxCDReconciliationFailure, which will be triggered if the rate of reconciliation failures in the flux-system namespace exceeds 0 for 10 minutes. You can customize the alert expression, duration, and severity based on your requirements.

Apply the PrometheusRule Resource

Apply the flux-alerts.yaml file to your Kubernetes cluster:

```
kubectl apply -f flux-alerts.yaml
```

Configure Alertmanager to Send Notifications

You'll need to configure Alertmanager to send notifications when alerts are triggered. This involves editing the Alertmanager configuration, typically located in a ConfigMap or Secret. Refer to the Alertmanager documentation for instructions on configuring various receivers like email, Slack, or PagerDuty.

Verify Monitoring and Alerting

To verify that monitoring and alerting are working correctly, you can use the Prometheus web UI to explore the FluxCD metrics and check if the ServiceMonitor is correctly scraping the data. Access the Prometheus web UI by port-forwarding the Prometheus service or by exposing it through an Ingress resource.

```
kubectl -n <PROMETHEUS_NAMESPACE> port-forward svc/prometheus-kube-prometheus-prometheus 9090:9090
```

Replace <PROMETHEUS_NAMESPACE> with the namespace where you have installed Prometheus (usually monitoring or prometheus).

Once you have access to the Prometheus web UI, you can search for FluxCD-specific metrics (such as flux_reconcile_failure_count) and ensure they are being collected.

Next, navigate to the Alertmanager web UI to verify that your custom alerts have been loaded and are being evaluated. Access the Alertmanager web UI by port-forwarding the Alertmanager service or by exposing it through an Ingress resource.

```
kubectl -n <PROMETHEUS_NAMESPACE> port-forward svc/prometheus-kube-prometheus-alertmanager 9093:9093
```

Replace <PROMETHEUS_NAMESPACE> with the namespace where you have installed Prometheus.

In the Alertmanager web UI, you should see your custom alerts under the "Alerts" tab. If an alert is triggered, you should receive a notification through the configured receiver(s).

By following these steps, you can set up monitoring and alerting with FluxCD to keep an eye on your cluster's health, performance, and stability. This will enable you to react quickly to issues and maintain a reliable and efficient Kubernetes environment.

Advanced FluxCD Features

FluxCD offers several advanced features that allow you to further customize and enhance your GitOps workflow. Some of these features include:

Image Automation

FluxCD can automatically update your Kubernetes manifests when a new container image is available in a container registry. This can be achieved using ImageRepository and ImagePolicy custom resources, along with ImageUpdateAutomation resources to update the Git repository. With image automation, you can ensure that your applications always run the latest container images without manual intervention.

Notifications and Event Forwarding

FluxCD's notification-controller can send notifications to various channels like Slack, Microsoft Teams, Discord, and others when specific events occur. You can configure the notification-controller using Alert and Provider custom resources. Additionally, you can forward events to external systems like Elasticsearch, Sentry, or custom APIs using Event and Receiver custom resources. This enables you to better integrate FluxCD with your existing monitoring and alerting infrastructure.

Multi-tenancy

FluxCD supports multi-tenancy, allowing you to manage multiple tenants within a single Kubernetes cluster. Each tenant can have its own Git repository, FluxCD instance, and restricted access to specific namespaces or clusters. This enables you to isolate tenants' resources and configurations and enforce strict access control policies.

Health Checks and Dependencies

FluxCD can perform health checks on your applications after a reconciliation. It uses Kubernetes' built-in health checks (liveness and readiness probes) to determine if an application is healthy after an update. Additionally, you can define dependencies between applications, ensuring that they are updated in the correct order. This is particularly useful when you have applications that depend on other services or configurations to be deployed first.

Garbage Collection

FluxCD can automatically remove Kubernetes resources that are no longer present in the Git repository. This feature, known as garbage collection, helps keep your cluster clean and prevents orphaned resources from consuming resources and causing conflicts. Garbage collection can be enabled on a per-namespace or global basis.

Cluster API Support

FluxCD has built-in support for managing Kubernetes clusters using the Cluster API (CAPI). With this integration, you can manage the lifecycle of your Kubernetes clusters using GitOps, including provisioning, scaling, and upgrading. This allows you to treat your cluster infrastructure as code, ensuring that your infrastructure is versioned, auditable, and easily recoverable.

These advanced features, combined with FluxCD's core functionality, provide a comprehensive and flexible GitOps solution for managing Kubernetes applications and infrastructure. By utilizing these features, you can further optimize your development and deployment workflows, enhance security and compliance, and better integrate FluxCD with your existing toolchain.

Summary

FluxCD is an open-source tool that follows GitOps principles to automate software delivery pipelines. It ensures the consistency of the desired state of Kubernetes cluster resources and applications by continuously syncing with Git repositories. GitOps principles enable developers to manage infrastructure as code, review changes through pull requests, and track the history of changes using Git. The GitOps workflow involves a developer pushing code changes to a Git repository, triggering a build and deployment process in a continuous integration/continuous deployment (CI/CD) pipeline, and finally, the deployment is synced with the Kubernetes cluster using FluxCD.

Installing and configuring FluxCD involves installing the FluxCD operator and configuring the Git repository that contains the Kubernetes manifests. The FluxCD operator is a Kubernetes controller that listens to changes in Git repositories and updates the cluster's state accordingly. The configuration of the Git repository includes defining the branch, path, and interval for FluxCD to check for changes. Continuous delivery with FluxCD is achieved by automating the entire deployment process, including building, testing, and releasing software changes. FluxCD monitors the Git repository for changes and applies those changes to the cluster, ensuring that the latest version of the application is running on the cluster.

Managing secrets and configmaps with FluxCD involves using Kubernetes secrets and configmaps to manage sensitive data and configuration variables, respectively. FluxCD can automate the creation and management of secrets and configmaps by syncing them with the Git repository. Monitoring and logging with FluxCD can be achieved by integrating FluxCD with other monitoring and logging tools, such as Prometheus and Grafana. This integration enables developers to monitor the performance of their applications, track changes in the Kubernetes cluster, and diagnose and troubleshoot issues.

Finally, advanced FluxCD features include support for Helm charts, multi-tenancy, and canary releases. Helm charts are a package manager for Kubernetes that simplifies the deployment of complex applications. Multi-tenancy enables multiple teams to use a single Kubernetes cluster, while canary releases enable developers to release new features to a small subset of users for testing before rolling out the changes to the entire user base.

Chapter 4: Virtual Kubelet and Serverless Clusters

Introduction to Virtual Kubelet

Virtual Kubelet is an open-source Kubernetes kubelet implementation that extends the Kubernetes API to support adding nodes that don't necessarily run on a traditional VM, container, or bare-metal host. It acts as an interface between Kubernetes and other systems or platforms, allowing Kubernetes to manage workloads running outside the cluster, such as those running on serverless platforms, edge devices, or in other cloud providers.

In the context of multi-cloud Kubernetes, Virtual Kubelet provides the following benefits:

Seamless integration with serverless platforms:
Virtual Kubelet allows you to run Kubernetes workloads on serverless platforms like Azure Container Instances, AWS Fargate, or Google Cloud Run. This enables you to benefit from the scalability, cost-efficiency, and reduced operational overhead provided by these platforms while still using Kubernetes for workload management.

Multi-cloud workload distribution:
Virtual Kubelet enables you to distribute workloads across multiple cloud providers. You can run some workloads on traditional VMs, containers, or bare-metal hosts, while running others on serverless platforms or even other Kubernetes clusters. This helps optimize resource usage, cost, and performance, while also ensuring high availability and fault tolerance.

Simplified management of edge devices:
Virtual Kubelet can be used to manage workloads running on edge devices like IoT sensors, smart appliances, or gateways. This allows you to leverage Kubernetes' powerful management capabilities to deploy, scale, and monitor applications running on the edge, simplifying the management of these distributed systems.

Easier migration between cloud providers:
Using Virtual Kubelet, you can more easily migrate workloads between cloud providers or to on-premises environments. By abstracting the underlying infrastructure, Virtual Kubelet allows you to use the same Kubernetes manifests and workflows across different platforms, simplifying the migration process.

Extensibility and custom integrations:
Virtual Kubelet is designed to be extensible, allowing you to create custom providers to integrate with other platforms, services, or infrastructure that are not natively supported. This enables you to extend Kubernetes to manage a wide range of workloads and

environments, tailored to your specific needs.

Virtual Kubelet plays a crucial role in the context of multi-cloud Kubernetes by enabling seamless integration with various platforms and systems, simplifying workload management, and providing greater flexibility in workload distribution. This helps organizations optimize their infrastructure, reduce costs, and more effectively manage their applications across a diverse range of environments.

Integrate Virtual Kubelet with Multi-cloud

To integrate Virtual Kubelet with your multi-cloud environment consisting of AWS and GCP, you'll need to set up Virtual Kubelet to work with AWS Fargate and Google Cloud Run. This section will walk you through the process for both platforms.

Note: You need to have a Kubernetes cluster running on both AWS and GCP. This section assumes you have kubectl and helm installed and configured to work with your clusters.

Install Virtual Kubelet on Kubernetes Clusters

First, you need to install Virtual Kubelet on both your AWS and GCP Kubernetes clusters. You can use the official Helm chart to install Virtual Kubelet.

Add the Virtual Kubelet Helm repository:

```
helm repo add virtual-kubelet https://virtual-kubelet.github.io/charts
helm repo update
```

Configure Virtual Kubelet for AWS Fargate

To use Virtual Kubelet with AWS Fargate, you'll need to create an Amazon ECR repository to store your container images, create an IAM role with the necessary permissions, and configure Virtual Kubelet with the AWS provider.

Follow the official AWS Fargate provider guide to set up Virtual Kubelet for AWS Fargate.

Configure Virtual Kubelet for Google Cloud Run

To use Virtual Kubelet with Google Cloud Run, you'll need to enable the Cloud Run API, create a Google Cloud project, and configure Virtual Kubelet with the Cloud Run provider.

Follow the official Google Cloud Run provider guide to set up Virtual Kubelet for Google Cloud Run.

Deploy Workloads on AWS Fargate and Google Cloud Run

With Virtual Kubelet installed and configured for both AWS Fargate and Google Cloud Run, you can now deploy workloads to these platforms using standard Kubernetes manifests.

To deploy a workload on AWS Fargate, set the spec.nodeName field in your Kubernetes manifests to the name of the Virtual Kubelet node representing AWS Fargate.

```
apiVersion: v1
kind: Pod
metadata:
  name: my-aws-fargate-pod
spec:
  nodeName: virtual-kubelet-aws
  containers:
  - name: my-container
    image: my-ecr-repo/my-image:latest
```

Similarly, to deploy a workload on Google Cloud Run, set the spec.nodeName field in your Kubernetes manifests to the name of the Virtual Kubelet node representing Google Cloud Run.

```
apiVersion: v1
kind: Pod
metadata:
  name: my-gcp-cloudrun-pod
spec:
  nodeName: virtual-kubelet-gcp
  containers:
  - name: my-container
    image: gcr.io/my-gcp-project/my-image:latest
```

<u>Apply Manifests using kubectl</u>

```
kubectl apply -f my-aws-fargate-pod.yaml
kubectl apply -f my-gcp-cloudrun-pod.yaml
```

By following these steps, you can integrate Virtual Kubelet with your multi-cloud environment on AWS and GCP. This enables you to deploy and manage Kubernetes workloads across both platforms using a consistent workflow and leveraging the benefits of serverless

Deploying Serverless Clusters

Serverless clusters refer to a Kubernetes-like environment where you don't need to manage the underlying nodes or infrastructure. Instead, you rely on serverless platforms that abstract away the infrastructure management, allowing you to focus on deploying and managing your applications. Serverless platforms automatically scale the resources based on demand and only charge for the resources consumed by your applications, which can lead to cost savings and improved operational efficiency.

Virtual Kubelet enables you to create a serverless cluster experience by integrating serverless platforms such as AWS Fargate and Google Cloud Run with Kubernetes. This allows you to deploy Kubernetes workloads on these serverless platforms, taking advantage of their scalability, cost-efficiency, and reduced operational overhead.

To deploy a serverless cluster using Virtual Kubelet, follow the steps outlined below:

Set Up Kubernetes Cluster

Ensure that you have a Kubernetes cluster up and running on your preferred cloud provider or on-premises environment. This cluster will act as the control plane for managing your serverless workloads.

Install Virtual Kubelet on Kubernetes Cluster

Install Virtual Kubelet using Helm, as described in the previous section. Ensure that you've added the Virtual Kubelet Helm repository and updated your Helm repo.

Configure Virtual Kubelet for Serverless Platform

Depending on the serverless platform you want to use, follow the appropriate provider guide:
- For AWS Fargate, refer to the AWS Fargate provider guide.
- For Google Cloud Run, refer to the Google Cloud Run provider guide.

Deploy Workloads on Serverless Platform

With Virtual Kubelet installed and configured, you can deploy Kubernetes workloads on your chosen serverless platform. You need to set the spec.nodeName field in your Kubernetes manifests to the name of the Virtual Kubelet node representing the serverless platform.

For example, if you're using AWS Fargate:

```
apiVersion: v1
kind: Pod
metadata:
  name: my-serverless-pod
spec:
  nodeName: virtual-kubelet-aws
  containers:
  - name: my-container
    image: my-ecr-repo/my-image:latest
```

Apply Manifests using kubectl

```
kubectl apply -f my-serverless-pod.yaml
```

Deploy/Manage Clusters and Serverless Workloads

You can use standard Kubernetes tools like kubectl and the Kubernetes Dashboard to manage your serverless workloads. You can also monitor and set up alerts using tools like Prometheus and Grafana.

By following these steps, you can create a serverless cluster experience using Virtual

Kubelet and your preferred serverless platform. This allows you to deploy and manage Kubernetes workloads on serverless platforms, enjoying the benefits of their scalability, cost-efficiency, and reduced operational overhead.

Scaling and Autoscaling with Virtual Kubelet

Manual and automatic scaling with Virtual Kubelet can be achieved through the use of Kubernetes' built-in features, such as ReplicaSet, Deployment, and the HorizontalPodAutoscaler. Virtual Kubelet delegates the scaling tasks to the serverless platforms it is integrated with, such as AWS Fargate or Google Cloud Run.

Manual Scaling

Manual scaling can be done using ReplicaSet or Deployment resources in Kubernetes. These resources allow you to specify the number of replicas you want for a given application.

Create Deployment

Create a Deployment that targets the Virtual Kubelet node representing your serverless platform by adding a nodeName field to the Pod spec:

```
apiVersion: apps/v1
kind: Deployment
metadata:
  name: my-serverless-app
spec:
  replicas: 3
  selector:
    matchLabels:
      app: my-serverless-app
  template:
    metadata:
      labels:
        app: my-serverless-app
    spec:
      nodeName: virtual-kubelet-aws  # or virtual-kubelet-gcp
```

```
    containers:
    - name: my-container
      image: my-ecr-repo/my-image:latest
```

Apply Deployment using kubectl

```
kubectl apply -f my-serverless-deployment.yaml
```

To manually scale the number of replicas, use the kubectl scale command:

```
kubectl scale deployment my-serverless-app --replicas=5
```

This command increases the number of replicas to 5.

Automatic Scaling

Automatic scaling can be achieved using the HorizontalPodAutoscaler (HPA) resource in Kubernetes. HPA automatically adjusts the number of replicas based on the observed CPU utilization or custom metrics.

First, ensure that the metrics-server is installed and running in your Kubernetes cluster. The metrics-server is required for the HPA to collect CPU and memory utilization data.

Create a HorizontalPodAutoscaler resource targeting your Deployment

```
apiVersion: autoscaling/v2beta2
kind: HorizontalPodAutoscaler
metadata:
  name: my-serverless-app-hpa
spec:
  scaleTargetRef:
    apiVersion: apps/v1
    kind: Deployment
    name: my-serverless-app
  minReplicas: 1
```

```yaml
  maxReplicas: 10
  metrics:
  - type: Resource
    resource:
      name: cpu
      target:
        type: Utilization
        averageUtilization: 50
```

This HPA configuration will try to maintain an average CPU utilization of 50% across all replicas, scaling the number of replicas between 1 and 10 as needed.

Apply the HorizontalPodAutoscaler using kubectl

```
kubectl apply -f my-serverless-hpa.yaml
```

With these configurations, you can manually and automatically scale your workloads running on serverless platforms using Virtual Kubelet. The scaling tasks are delegated to the serverless platforms, ensuring that your applications are efficiently scaled based on demand.

Monitoring and Logging in Serverless Clusters

Monitoring and logging in serverless clusters using Virtual Kubelet can be achieved using Prometheus for metrics collection and a logging solution like Elasticsearch, Fluentd, and Kibana (EFK) or Loki for log aggregation and analysis.

In this section, we'll focus on setting up Prometheus for monitoring serverless clusters. Keep in mind that monitoring serverless platforms might be different from monitoring traditional Kubernetes nodes since the underlying infrastructure is abstracted away.

Monitoring with Prometheus

Install Prometheus in your Kubernetes cluster: You can use the kube-prometheus-stack Helm chart to deploy Prometheus, Grafana, Alertmanager, and related exporters in your cluster.

Add the Prometheus Community Helm repository and install the chart:

```
helm repo add prometheus-community https://prometheus-
community.github.io/helm-charts
helm repo update
helm install my-prometheus prometheus-community/kube-prometheus-stack
```

Configure Prometheus to scrape metrics from Virtual Kubelet: Virtual Kubelet exposes metrics in the Prometheus format on the /metrics endpoint. You need to configure Prometheus to scrape these metrics.

Create a ServiceMonitor resource that targets the Virtual Kubelet nodes:

```
apiVersion: monitoring.coreos.com/v1
kind: ServiceMonitor
metadata:
  name: virtual-kubelet
  labels:
    release: my-prometheus
spec:
  selector:
    matchLabels:
      app: virtual-kubelet
  endpoints:
  - port: metrics
    interval: 15s
```

Apply the ServiceMonitor using kubectl:

```
kubectl apply -f virtual-kubelet-servicemonitor.yaml
```

Visualize Metrics with Grafana

The kube-prometheus-stack chart includes Grafana for visualizing metrics. Access the Grafana dashboard by port-forwarding the Grafana service:

```
kubectl port-forward svc/my-prometheus-grafana 3000:80
```

Open your browser and navigate to http://localhost:3000. Use the default credentials (username: admin, password: prom-operator) to log in. You can now create custom dashboards to visualize the metrics from your serverless clusters running on Virtual Kubelet.

Logging with EFK or Loki

Setting up a logging solution for serverless clusters with Virtual Kubelet might require you to use the native logging solutions provided by the serverless platforms, such as AWS CloudWatch Logs for AWS Fargate or Google Cloud Logging for Google Cloud Run.

However, you can still collect logs from your applications by configuring Fluentd or Fluent Bit to forward logs to Elasticsearch or Loki. You can then use Kibana or Grafana to visualize and analyze the logs. Refer to the official documentation for setting up EFK or Loki in your Kubernetes cluster.

By following these steps, you can set up monitoring and logging for your serverless clusters using Virtual Kubelet, allowing you to gain insights into your applications' performance and troubleshoot issues.

Summary

We discussed the concept of Virtual Kubelet and its benefits in the context of multi-cloud environments. Virtual Kubelet is a tool that allows for the integration of various cloud providers such as Amazon Web Services (AWS) and Google Cloud Platform (GCP) into a single Kubernetes cluster, making it easier to deploy and manage applications in a hybrid or multi-cloud environment.

To use Virtual Kubelet with multi-cloud providers, first, you need to create a Kubernetes cluster and configure it with Virtual Kubelet. Next, you can deploy serverless clusters using services like AWS Fargate or Google Cloud Run. Virtual Kubelet allows for scaling and autoscaling of these serverless clusters based on the demand of the application, reducing costs and ensuring high availability. Virtual Kubelet also provides monitoring and logging capabilities, allowing you to monitor the health and performance of your applications running in the hybrid or multi-cloud environment. The Virtual Kubelet system sends metrics to a monitoring system like Prometheus or Datadog, and logs can be sent to centralized logging solutions such as Elasticsearch or Splunk.

In summary, Virtual Kubelet is a powerful tool that can help you integrate multiple cloud providers into a single Kubernetes cluster, allowing you to deploy and manage applications more efficiently in a hybrid or multi-cloud environment. By deploying serverless clusters with Virtual Kubelet, you can scale and autoscale based on application demand and reduce costs while ensuring high availability. Virtual Kubelet also provides monitoring and logging capabilities, allowing you to keep track of your applications' health and performance across different cloud providers.

Chapter 5:
Networking with Submariner

Introduction to Submariner

Submariner is an open-source, Kubernetes-native networking solution designed to enable seamless and secure interconnectivity between Kubernetes clusters across multiple clouds, data centers, and geographies. It provides a consistent and unified experience for developers and administrators, regardless of the underlying infrastructure. In today's world, where applications and services span across various cloud providers and on-premise environments, Submariner plays a crucial role in simplifying the management of multi-cloud Kubernetes deployments.

Key Features

Secure Inter-Cluster Communication: Submariner provides secure, encrypted communication between Kubernetes clusters, ensuring that your sensitive data remains protected while traversing the internet or other insecure networks. This is particularly important for multi-cloud environments where data travels between clusters hosted on different cloud providers.

Network Discovery and Routing: Submariner automatically discovers and connects clusters and their networks, enabling seamless inter-cluster communication. It uses a dedicated Gateway node in each cluster to establish and manage secure tunnels between clusters. This simplifies the process of connecting disparate clusters and reduces administrative overhead.

Cross-Cluster Service Discovery: Submariner extends the native Kubernetes service discovery capabilities to work across multiple clusters. It enables Kubernetes services to be accessible and discoverable from other clusters within the connected environment, promoting a seamless and consistent experience for developers and users.

Load Balancing and High Availability: Submariner integrates with Kubernetes' native load balancing and traffic management features, ensuring that traffic is efficiently distributed across available resources, even when they are spread across different clusters or cloud providers. This helps to optimize resource utilization, improve application performance, and enhance the overall reliability of your multi-cloud deployments.

Network Policy Support: Submariner extends Kubernetes' native network policy support to work across clusters, enabling you to enforce consistent security and access control policies for your applications and services, regardless of their location.

Integration with Existing Networking Solutions: Submariner is designed to work alongside existing networking solutions such as Calico, Flannel, and others. It also supports multiple CNI (Container Network Interface) plugins, allowing you to leverage the best tools for your specific requirements.

Platform Agnostic: Submariner is compatible with a wide range of Kubernetes platforms, including major cloud providers like AWS, Google Cloud, Azure, and on-premise solutions like VMware and OpenShift. This ensures that you can benefit from Submariner's features, regardless of your chosen infrastructure.

Why Submariner for Multi-cloud Kubernetes

Simplified Management: Submariner simplifies the management of multi-cloud Kubernetes deployments by automating much of the process of connecting and managing disparate clusters. This allows you to focus on building and deploying your applications, rather than wrestling with complex networking challenges.

Consistent Application Experience: By enabling seamless inter-cluster communication and service discovery, Submariner promotes a consistent experience for your applications and services, regardless of where they are deployed. This ensures that your users receive a reliable, high-quality experience, even as your infrastructure evolves and grows.

Improved Security: Submariner's secure, encrypted communication channels protect your sensitive data as it travels between clusters, ensuring that it remains safe from eavesdropping and tampering. This is particularly important in multi-cloud environments where data often traverses less secure networks.

Enhanced Resilience and Scalability: Submariner's support for load balancing and high availability ensures that your applications remain performant and resilient, even as they scale across multiple clusters and cloud providers. This helps to ensure that your infrastructure can grow and adapt to meet the needs of your users and your business.

Cost Optimization: By enabling seamless interconnectivity between clusters hosted on different cloud providers, Submariner allows you to take advantage of the best pricing, features, and services offered by each provider. This helps you optimize costs and avoid vendor lock-in, ensuring that your multi-cloud Kubernetes deployment remains flexible and cost-effective.

Streamlined Compliance and Security: Submariner's support for network policies across multiple clusters simplifies the process of enforcing consistent security and access control rules for your applications and services. This is particularly important in regulated industries, where maintaining compliance across different environments can be challenging.

Rapid Innovation: Submariner's platform-agnostic design and compatibility with a wide range of Kubernetes platforms and networking solutions ensure that you can leverage the latest innovations and technologies in the Kubernetes ecosystem. This helps you stay at the cutting edge of cloud-native development, giving you a competitive advantage in the rapidly-evolving world of multi-cloud deployments.

Overall, Submariner is a powerful and versatile networking solution designed to simplify the management and operation of multi-cloud Kubernetes deployments. Its core features, such as secure inter-cluster communication, network discovery and routing, cross-cluster service discovery, load balancing, high availability, and network policy support, make it an essential tool for organizations looking to deploy and manage applications across multiple clouds and data centers. By reducing the complexity of multi-cloud networking, Submariner enables you to focus on what truly matters: building and deploying innovative applications and services that delight your users and drive your business forward.

Installing and Configuring Submariner

To deploy Submariner in a multi-cloud setup involving AWS and GCP, the following steps should be taken. It is assumed that Kubernetes clusters are already up and running on both cloud providers and that the necessary command-line tools (aws and gcloud) and kubectl are installed.

Install Subctl

Subctl is a powerful command-line utility that simplifies the deployment and management of Submariner, a tool that provides cross-cluster network connectivity for Kubernetes. With subctl, users can easily deploy and manage Submariner across their clusters without having to manually configure network connectivity.

The subctl utility is designed to streamline the process of deploying Submariner by automating many of the tasks involved. For example, subctl can automatically detect the various clusters in a user's environment and configure the necessary components for Submariner to work seamlessly across them. It can also handle the deployment and management of the various Submariner components, including the Broker, Gateway, and Route Agent.

Furthermore, subctl provides a simple and intuitive interface for managing Submariner. Users can easily check the status of their Submariner deployment, view logs, and perform various administrative tasks using the subctl command-line tool.

Install it using the following commands:

```
VERSION=$(curl --silent https://get.submariner.io/releases/latest/version)
curl -L https://get.submariner.io/releases/${VERSION}/subctl-${VERSION}-
linux-amd64.tar.xz | tar -xJf -
sudo mv subctl-*-linux-amd64/subctl /usr/local/bin/subctl
rm -rf subctl-*-linux-amd64
```

Replace "linux" with "darwin" for macOS or "windows" for Windows in the download URL.

Prepare AWS and GCP Clusters

In order to deploy Submariner successfully, it is important to verify that the Kubernetes clusters in both AWS and GCP are properly configured with the necessary network settings. This involves checking that the clusters have the correct subnets, security groups, and routing configurations in place. Without these configurations, Submariner may not function properly or could encounter connectivity issues between the clusters. Therefore, it is crucial to ensure that all necessary network configurations are in place before deploying Submariner in a multicloud Kubernetes environment as below:

AWS
- VPC peering or VPN connection between the VPCs hosting the clusters
- Security groups configured to allow IPsec traffic

GCP
- VPC Network Peering or VPN connection between the VPCs hosting the clusters
- Firewall rules configured to allow IPsec traffic

Note: Refer to your cloud provider's documentation for setting up peering or VPN connections and configuring security groups or firewall rules.

Export KUBECONFIG Files

To ensure proper communication with multiple Kubernetes clusters, it is essential to set the KUBECONFIG environment variable correctly. This variable specifies the configuration file(s) that kubectl uses to connect to the cluster. You can merge multiple KUBECONFIG files into a single file or use separate files for each cluster. This provides flexibility in managing and accessing multiple clusters with a single kubectl installation. By configuring KUBECONFIG, you can avoid errors and issues that may arise due to incorrect connection settings. Properly setting up KUBECONFIG is a crucial step in the process of managing multiple Kubernetes clusters.

For example, if you have separate KUBECONFIG files for AWS and GCP:

```
export KUBECONFIG_AWS=path/to/aws-kubeconfig.yaml
export KUBECONFIG_GCP=path/to/gcp-kubeconfig.yaml
```

Deploy Submariner

To deploy Submariner on multiple clusters, you can use subctl. The first step is to replace the placeholders "CLUSTER_NAME" and "BROKER" with the relevant values. The broker cluster is usually one of the participating clusters, but it can also be a separate cluster. Subctl is a command-line tool that simplifies the deployment and management of Submariner, a solution for connecting Kubernetes clusters. By using subctl, you can ensure that your Submariner deployment is consistent and reliable across all clusters. Once Submariner is deployed, you can start exploring its features such as cross-cluster service discovery and load balancing.

AWS

```
export KUBECONFIG=$KUBECONFIG_AWS
subctl join --kubeconfig $KUBECONFIG_AWS --clusterid aws-cluster --
natt=false --cable-driver aws-ec2 path/to/broker-kubeconfig.yaml
```

GCP

```
export KUBECONFIG=$KUBECONFIG_GCP
subctl join --kubeconfig $KUBECONFIG_GCP --clusterid gcp-cluster --
natt=false --cable-driver libreswan path/to/broker-kubeconfig.yaml
```

The --natt=false flag disables NAT traversal for IPsec, which is not required when peering or VPN connections are used.

Verify Submariner Deployment

To ensure that Submariner has been successfully deployed, one can use the subctl tool. This tool provides a simple and efficient way to check the status of Submariner components and resources:

```
subctl show all --kubeconfig path/to/broker-kubeconfig.yaml
```

You should see the clusters, endpoints, and gateways for both AWS and GCP.

Test Connectivity

Deploy a test application on each cluster and expose it as a Kubernetes service. Then, use the exported service's DNS name or IP address to test connectivity between the clusters.

For example, deploy an NGINX service on the AWS cluster and a Busybox pod on the GCP cluster. From the Busybox pod, use `wgetorcurlto test connectivity to the NGINX service on the AWS cluster. Replace<nginx-service-dns>` with the appropriate DNS name or IP address of the NGINX service:

```
# On AWS cluster
kubectl run nginx --image=nginx --port=80 --expose

# On GCP cluster
kubectl run busybox --image=busybox --rm -it --restart=Never -- sh

# From the Busybox pod
wget -qO- http://<nginx-service-dns>:80
```

If the connectivity test is successful, you should see the default NGINX welcome page content in the Busybox pod.

With this, you have successfully installed and configured Submariner in a multi-cloud environment with AWS and GCP. Your Kubernetes clusters are now connected, and you can seamlessly deploy and manage applications across both cloud providers. Remember to configure your application deployments and services to make the most of Submariner's features, such as cross-cluster service discovery, load balancing, and network policy support.

Cross-cluster Networking with Submariner

Cross-cluster networking is a crucial aspect of multi-cloud and hybrid cloud setups that allow services and resources to communicate across different Kubernetes clusters. This is especially important when dealing with large-scale deployments that span across different regions or data centers. One of the tools that enable cross-cluster networking is Submariner. It offers a secure and seamless way to connect Kubernetes clusters and extends service discovery, networking, and load balancing capabilities across them. By using Submariner, organizations can ensure that their applications are running smoothly across different Kubernetes clusters, regardless of the cloud provider or data center. This allows for better scalability, fault-tolerance, and performance of applications running in multi-cloud or hybrid environments. With the increasing popularity of cloud-native applications, cross-cluster networking is becoming a critical aspect of infrastructure management, and tools like Submariner are essential for effective implementation.

Below is a step-by-step walkthrough on implementing cross-cluster networking using Submariner:

Create a Headless Service

To enable cross-cluster communication, the first step is to establish a headless service in the target cluster where the application you wish to expose is located. In Kubernetes, a headless service is a type of service that lacks a cluster IP, allowing you to expose your application's pods directly. This is essential for cross-cluster networking because it enables direct communication between the pods without any intermediary routing.

A headless service allows you to use Kubernetes DNS to access your application's pods. This means that the pods can be accessed by their unique DNS names, which are based on their pod names and the name of the headless service. This provides a consistent and reliable way to communicate with your pods, even if they move between nodes or clusters.

For example, let us see a simple Nginx deployment running in your target cluster:

```yaml
Copy code
apiVersion: apps/v1
kind: Deployment
metadata:
  name: nginx
```

```yaml
spec:
 replicas: 1
 selector:
  matchLabels:
   app: nginx
 template:
  metadata:
   labels:
    app: nginx
  spec:
   containers:
   - name: nginx
     image: nginx:1.14.2
     ports:
     - containerPort: 80
```

Create a headless service for the Nginx deployment

To establish a headless service for the Nginx deployment, you can create a Kubernetes service of the "ClusterIP" type with a selector that matches the label of the Nginx deployment. This will enable the service to locate and communicate with the Nginx pods. In addition, by setting the "clusterIP" field to "None," you can create a headless service that returns the IP addresses of the individual pods instead of a single IP address for the service. This approach can be useful when you need to target individual pods directly.

```yaml
apiVersion: v1
kind: Service
metadata:
 name: nginx-headless
spec:
 type: ClusterIP
 clusterIP: None
 ports:
 - name: http
```

    port: 80
selector:
  app: nginx

Apply the YAML manifest to create the headless service
To create a headless service using the YAML manifest, you can apply the necessary
configurations and settings. This process involves defining the metadata and specifications
for the headless service, including its name and selector. Once applied, the headless service
will be created and can be accessed by its name. This enables communication with
individual pods within a Kubernetes cluster without relying on a single IP address, making
it more resilient and scalable.

kubectl apply -f nginx-headless-service.yaml

Create SubmarinerExport Resource

In order to make the headless service easily discoverable from other clusters, it is
recommended to create a SubmarinerExport resource in the target cluster. This resource is
a customized element of the Submariner's Lighthouse project and is specifically designed
to export services across connected clusters. By creating this resource, the headless service
can be accessed from other clusters in a seamless manner, ensuring smooth functioning of
the entire cluster network.

The SubmarinerExport resource is a crucial tool for any organization that relies on multiple
clusters for their operations. By using this resource, administrators can export services from
one cluster to another and ensure that they are easily discoverable across different clusters.
This is particularly important for headless services that may be required to communicate
with other services or applications located in different clusters.

apiVersion: lighthouse.submariner.io/v2alpha1
kind: ServiceExport
metadata:
  name: nginx-headless
  namespace: default

Apply the YAML manifest to create the ServiceExport resource
To create a ServiceExport resource, you can apply the YAML manifest that specifies the

desired configuration. This will define the exported service and make it available across multiple clusters in a multicloud setup. By doing this, you can ensure that the service is accessible across all clusters, regardless of the cloud provider they are running on. The ServiceExport resource can be a valuable tool for managing and scaling your Kubernetes cluster.

```
kubectl apply -f nginx-headless-export.yaml
```

Access Service from Another Cluster

After exporting the headless service, you can access it from another connected cluster using its DNS name. The format of the DNS name is <service-name>.<namespace>.svc.clusterset.local. For our example, the DNS name would be nginx-headless.default.svc.clusterset.local.

To test the connectivity, deploy a Busybox pod in the source cluster and use wget or curl to access the Nginx service in the target cluster:

```
# On source cluster
kubectl run busybox --image=busybox --rm -it --restart=Never -- sh

# From the Busybox pod
wget -qO- http://nginx-headless.default.svc.clusterset.local:80
```

If the connectivity test is successful, you should see the default Nginx welcome page content in the Busybox pod.

You have now successfully implemented cross-cluster networking using Submariner. Your Kubernetes resources can communicate across clusters, allowing you to deploy and manage applications seamlessly across multiple environments. This capability simplifies application development and management, as well as enabling advanced use cases like disaster

Service Discovery

Service discovery is the process by which applications and services within a distributed system can locate and communicate with each other. In Kubernetes, service discovery is typically achieved through the use of Kubernetes services, which provide stable IP addresses and DNS names to reach the underlying application Pods.

Submariner extends the native Kubernetes service discovery capabilities to work across multiple connected clusters. It allows services to be accessible and discoverable from other clusters within the connected environment, making it easier to manage and scale applications across different clusters or cloud providers.

Below is a step-by-step walkthrough on implementing cross-cluster service discovery using Submariner:

Create Kubernetes Service

To demonstrate cross-cluster service discovery, let us look at a scenario wherein you have a simple Nginx deployment running in your target cluster:

```
apiVersion: apps/v1
kind: Deployment
metadata:
  name: nginx
spec:
  replicas: 1
  selector:
    matchLabels:
      app: nginx
  template:
    metadata:
      labels:
        app: nginx
    spec:
      containers:
      - name: nginx
        image: nginx:1.14.2
        ports:
        - containerPort: 80
```

Create a Kubernetes service for the Nginx deployment

```yaml
apiVersion: v1
kind: Service
metadata:
  name: nginx-service
spec:
  selector:
    app: nginx
  ports:
    - protocol: TCP
      port: 80
      targetPort: 80
```

Apply the YAML manifest to create the service

```
kubectl apply -f nginx-service.yaml
```

Export the Service

To make the Kubernetes service discoverable from other clusters, create a ServiceExport resource in the target cluster. This custom resource is part of the Submariner's Lighthouse project and helps export services across connected clusters.

```yaml
apiVersion: lighthouse.submariner.io/v2alpha1
kind: ServiceExport
metadata:
  name: nginx-service
  namespace: default
```

Apply the YAML manifest to create the ServiceExport resource

```
kubectl apply -f nginx-service-export.yaml
```

<u># Discover Service from Another Cluster</u>

After exporting the service, you can access it from another connected cluster using its DNS name. The format of the DNS name is <service-name>.<namespace>.svc.clusterset.local. For our example, the DNS name would be nginx-service.default.svc.clusterset.local.

To test the service discovery, deploy a Busybox pod in the source cluster and use wget or curl to access the Nginx service in the target cluster:

```
# On source cluster
kubectl run busybox --image=busybox --rm -it --restart=Never -- sh

# From the Busybox pod
wget -qO- http://nginx-service.default.svc.clusterset.local:80
```

If the service discovery test is successful, you should see the default Nginx welcome page content in the Busybox pod.

You have now successfully implemented cross-cluster service discovery using Submariner. Your Kubernetes services are discoverable across clusters, allowing you to deploy and manage applications seamlessly across multiple environments. This capability simplifies application development and management, as well as enabling advanced use cases like disaster recovery, load balancing, and multi-cloud deployments.

Load Balancing

Load balancing is an essential aspect of any Kubernetes environment, as it ensures that network traffic is distributed evenly across multiple application instances (Pods) for better availability, fault tolerance, and optimal resource utilization. Kubernetes offers in-built support for load balancing through its Services, which provides a stable entry point for accessing the underlying application Pods. However, in a multi-cluster Kubernetes environment, it is important to ensure that traffic is not only balanced within a single cluster but also across multiple connected clusters. This is where Submariner comes into play. Submariner is an open-source networking solution that enables cross-cluster connectivity and service discovery in Kubernetes. It provides a seamless way to connect multiple Kubernetes clusters and allows for traffic to be load-balanced across those clusters.

By leveraging the built-in Kubernetes load balancing capabilities with Submariner, you can distribute traffic across multiple clusters in a transparent and consistent manner. This means that applications can be deployed across multiple clusters and still be accessed using a single stable endpoint, improving the overall user experience. Furthermore, by utilizing Submariner's load balancing capabilities, you can also ensure that your applications are highly available and fault-tolerant, even in the event of failures within a cluster or network disruption.

Below is a step-by-step walkthrough on implementing cross-cluster load balancing using Submariner:

Deploy Application in Multiple Clusters

To demonstrate cross-cluster load balancing, deploy the same application (e.g., Nginx) in multiple connected clusters. In each cluster, create a Deployment and a Service for the application.

For example, create the following Nginx Deployment and Service manifests for each cluster:

Nginx Deployment

```
apiVersion: apps/v1
kind: Deployment
metadata:
  name: nginx
spec:
  replicas: 2
  selector:
    matchLabels:
      app: nginx
  template:
    metadata:
      labels:
        app: nginx
    spec:
      containers:
      - name: nginx
```

```yaml
    image: nginx:1.14.2
    ports:
    - containerPort: 80
```

Nginx Service

```yaml
apiVersion: v1
kind: Service
metadata:
  name: nginx-service
spec:
  selector:
    app: nginx
  ports:
    - protocol: TCP
      port: 80
      targetPort: 80
```

Apply the YAML manifests to create the Deployment and Service in each cluster

```
kubectl apply -f nginx-deployment.yaml
kubectl apply -f nginx-service.yaml
```

Export the Services

In each cluster, create a ServiceExport resource for the Nginx Service to make it discoverable from other connected clusters:

```yaml
apiVersion: lighthouse.submariner.io/v2alpha1
kind: ServiceExport
metadata:
  name: nginx-service
  namespace: default
```

```
kubectl apply -f nginx-service-export.yaml
```

Access Service from Another Cluster

After exporting the Services, you can access them from any connected cluster using the DNS name <service-name>.<namespace>.svc.clusterset.local. In the below demonstrated example, the DNS name is nginx-service.default.svc.clusterset.local.

Since multiple clusters have the same service exported, Submariner will load balance the traffic across these services in different clusters. You can test this by deploying a Busybox pod in a source cluster and repeatedly using wget or curl to access the Nginx service.

```
# On source cluster
kubectl run busybox --image=busybox --rm -it --restart=Never -- sh
```

```
# From the Busybox pod
for i in {1..10}; do wget -qO- http://nginx-
service.default.svc.clusterset.local:80; done
```

If load balancing is working correctly, you should see responses from different Nginx instances in the various clusters.

You have now successfully implemented cross-cluster load balancing using Submariner. Your application traffic is distributed across multiple clusters, ensuring high availability, fault tolerance, and optimal resource utilization. This capability is crucial for building scalable and resilient applications in a multi-cluster or multi-cloud environment

Monitoring and Troubleshooting

Monitoring and troubleshooting are essential aspects of managing Kubernetes clusters, especially in multi-cluster environments. Submariner provides various tools and resources to help you monitor the health of your connected clusters and diagnose any issues that may arise.

Below are some ways to perform monitoring and troubleshooting with Submariner:

Monitor Submariner Components

Submariner deploys several components like Gateway Engine, Route Agent, and Lighthouse Agent in your Kubernetes clusters. You can monitor the health and status of these components using Kubernetes native tools like kubectl.

Check the status of Submariner components

```
kubectl -n submariner-operator get pods
```

Inspect logs of a specific component to identify issues

```
kubectl -n submariner-operator logs <pod-name>
```

Check Submariner Status

Submariner provides a subctl command-line tool that offers various commands to manage and monitor your connected clusters. You can use subctl to check the overall status of Submariner components and connections.

First, download the subctl binary from the Submariner GitHub repository:

```
curl -Ls https://get.submariner.io | bash
export PATH=$PATH:~/.local/bin
```

Then, use subctl show commands to check the status of various Submariner components:

```
subctl show all            # Show the status of all components
subctl show connections    # Show the status of Submariner connections
subctl show endpoints      # Show the status of Submariner endpoints
subctl show gateways       # Show the status of Submariner gateways
subctl show networks       # Show the status of cluster networks
subctl show serviceexports # Show the status of exported services
```

Use Submariner Metrics

Submariner exports Prometheus metrics that can be used to monitor the performance and health of your connected clusters. You can set up a monitoring stack with tools like Prometheus and Grafana to collect, store, visualize, and alert on these metrics.

To enable metrics, you need to deploy the Submariner Operator with the --metrics flag:

```
subctl deploy-broker --kubeconfig broker-kubeconfig.yaml --metrics
```

Configure your Prometheus instance to scrape metrics from the Submariner Gateway Engine and Route Agent:

```
scrape_configs:
  - job_name: 'submariner'
    static_configs:
    - targets: ['<gateway-engine-ip>:8080', '<route-agent-ip>:8080']
```

You can find the list of available Submariner metrics in the official documentation.

Troubleshoot Connectivity Issues

If you encounter connectivity issues between your connected clusters, you can use subctl to diagnose and troubleshoot the problem.

Run subctl validate to check various aspects of your connected clusters, such as the Kubernetes version, CNI configuration, and Submariner components:

```
subctl validate all
```

Use subctl test to perform end-to-end connectivity tests between your clusters:

```
subctl test connections
```

These tools, along with the standard Kubernetes monitoring and troubleshooting practices, will help you maintain the health and performance of your Submariner-enabled multi-cluster environment. Remember to keep an eye on the logs, metrics, and connectivity tests to ensure that your connected clusters are functioning optimally.

Summary

In this chapter, we discussed various aspects of Submariner, a network connectivity solution for Kubernetes clusters, particularly in multi-cloud environments. Submariner extends Kubernetes' native networking capabilities, allowing seamless communication between different clusters regardless of their location. This solution offers a range of features, such as encrypted tunnels, cross-cluster service discovery, and load balancing.

We first covered how to install and configure Submariner in a multi-cloud environment, using AWS and GCP as examples. To do this, you need to prepare your Kubernetes clusters, create a Submariner broker, join your clusters to the broker, and verify the connectivity.

Next, we discussed cross-cluster networking, which enables services and resources in one cluster to communicate with those in another. Submariner facilitates this communication by providing a secure way to connect Kubernetes clusters and extend service discovery, networking, and load balancing capabilities across them. We covered the process of creating a headless service, exporting it using a ServiceExport resource, and accessing it from another cluster.

We then explored service discovery, the process by which applications and services within a distributed system can locate and communicate with each other. Submariner extends Kubernetes service discovery to work across multiple connected clusters, allowing services to be accessible and discoverable from other clusters within the connected environment. We went through the steps of creating a Kubernetes service, exporting it with a ServiceExport resource, and discovering it from another cluster.

Following that, we discussed implementing cross-cluster load balancing with Submariner. Load balancing is the process of distributing network traffic across multiple application instances (Pods) to ensure high availability and optimal resource utilization. By leveraging Kubernetes' built-in load balancing capabilities and Submariner's cross-cluster service discovery, we can distribute traffic across multiple connected clusters. We covered deploying the application in multiple clusters, exporting the services, and accessing them from another cluster.

Finally, we talked about monitoring and troubleshooting Submariner. Monitoring the health of your connected clusters and diagnosing any issues is critical in managing Kubernetes clusters, especially in multi-cluster environments. We discussed various ways to monitor and troubleshoot Submariner, such as checking the status of Submariner components, using the subctl command-line tool to monitor various aspects of Submariner, setting up a monitoring stack with tools like Prometheus and Grafana to collect and visualize metrics, and troubleshooting connectivity issues with subctl.

CHAPTER 6: MULTICLUSTER MANAGEMENT AND FEDERATION

Overview of MultiCluster Kubernetes

Multi-cluster in multi-cloud Kubernetes refers to a setup where Kubernetes clusters are distributed across multiple cloud providers or data centers, creating a unified platform for managing workloads and resources. In such a setup, each Kubernetes cluster runs independently in its respective environment, but they are interconnected and managed as a single logical entity. This architecture allows organizations to build and deploy applications that span multiple cloud providers or regions, ensuring high availability, fault tolerance, and optimal resource utilization.

Below is a detailed overview of multi-cluster, multi-cloud Kubernetes:

Advantages of Multi-Cluster, Multi-cloud Kubernetes

There are numerous advantages to using a multi-cluster, multi-cloud Kubernetes architecture for application deployment and management. Some of the key benefits include:

High Availability

By distributing applications and resources across multiple clusters and cloud providers, you reduce the risk of downtime caused by outages or failures in a single cloud provider or region.
Disaster Recovery: In the event of a catastrophic failure, a multi-cluster, multi-cloud setup ensures that you can easily failover to another cluster or cloud provider, minimizing the impact on your applications.

Data Locality

Deploying applications in multiple clusters, closer to your end-users, helps to reduce latency and improve the user experience.

Scalability

Multi-cluster, multi-cloud Kubernetes allows you to leverage the compute and storage resources of multiple cloud providers, helping you scale applications horizontally and vertically.

Flexibility

You can choose the best cloud provider, service, or infrastructure for each workload, avoiding vendor lock-in and optimizing your infrastructure costs.

Compliance

Deploying applications in multiple clusters and regions can help meet data residency and compliance requirements.

Challenges in Multi-Cluster, Multi-cloud Kubernetes

Multi-cluster, multi-cloud Kubernetes presents unique challenges that organizations must overcome to operate effectively in a hybrid cloud environment. In this expanded summary, we will delve deeper into the five main challenges mentioned earlier.

Networking

One of the primary challenges in multi-cluster, multi-cloud Kubernetes is establishing network connectivity between clusters in different cloud providers. Each provider has its own networking constructs and policies, which can make it challenging to ensure consistent communication between clusters. Organizations must implement a networking solution that can seamlessly connect clusters in different cloud providers while maintaining security and reliability.

Security

Security is another crucial challenge in multi-cluster, multi-cloud Kubernetes. Organizations must ensure secure communication between clusters and enforce consistent security policies across multiple environments. This requires implementing effective security measures such as encryption, access control, and network segmentation. The use of containerized applications also requires organizations to implement security measures that can protect against potential vulnerabilities and ensure compliance with regulatory requirements.

Service Discovery

Kubernetes native service discovery mechanisms do not work across multiple clusters, making it difficult to locate and access services running in different clusters. Organizations must implement service discovery solutions that can locate services running across different clusters and cloud providers. This requires additional tooling and configurations to ensure that services can be discovered and accessed seamlessly.

Load Balancing

Distributing traffic across multiple clusters and cloud providers requires additional configurations and tooling. Kubernetes native load balancing mechanisms work within a single cluster, making it challenging to distribute traffic across multiple clusters. Organizations must implement load balancing solutions that can distribute traffic effectively and efficiently across different clusters and cloud providers.

Configuration Management

Managing the configuration and deployment of applications across multiple clusters and cloud providers can be complex and error-prone. Organizations must implement effective configuration management tools and processes to manage configurations across different environments consistently. This requires automating the configuration management process, ensuring that all clusters are up to date, and monitoring the deployment of applications to ensure consistency and avoid errors.

Solutions for Multi-Cluster, Multi-cloud Kubernetes

In response to the complexity of managing multi-cluster, multi-cloud Kubernetes environments, various tools and projects have emerged. These solutions aim to simplify tasks such as deployment, scaling, and load balancing across different cloud providers, making it easier for organizations to manage their infrastructure.

Submariner

As discussed earlier in this chapter, Submariner is a network connectivity solution that provides secure communication between Kubernetes clusters, enabling cross-cluster service discovery, networking, and load balancing.

Rancher

Rancher is a complete container management platform that simplifies the deployment, management, and scaling of Kubernetes clusters across multiple cloud providers.

Google Anthos

Anthos is a hybrid and multi-cloud application platform that helps you modernize, build, and deploy applications across multiple environments, including on-premises and public cloud providers.

Kubernetes Federation (KubeFed)

KubeFed is a Kubernetes project that enables the management of multiple clusters through the synchronization of resources and configurations, providing a consistent experience across clusters.

In summary, multi-cluster, multi-cloud Kubernetes involves deploying and managing Kubernetes clusters across different cloud providers or data centers, enabling organizations to build and deploy applications that are highly available, fault-tolerant, and scalable. While there are challenges in managing multi-cluster, multi-cloud environments, several tools and projects exist to help overcome these hurdles and streamline the process.

Setup and Configure MultiCluster Federation

Before starting, ensure you have kubectl and kubefedctl installed on your machine. If you don't have kubefedctl, you can download the appropriate release from the KubeFed releases page.

Set up Kubernetes Clusters

To set up a federated Kubernetes cluster, it is essential to have access to at least two Kubernetes clusters that you want to federate. These clusters can be located on-premises or on different cloud providers, or a combination of both. To proceed, you need to ensure that you have the kubeconfig files for each cluster that you want to federate. The kubeconfig files will contain the necessary information that Kubernetes needs to communicate with each cluster.

For instance, if you have two clusters that you want to federate, and their respective kubeconfig files are named cluster1-kubeconfig.yaml and cluster2-kubeconfig.yaml, you can use these files to configure the Kubernetes federation control plane. With the configuration in place, you can begin deploying and managing applications across the federated clusters.

Deploy the KubeFed Control Plane

It is necessary to designate one of the clusters as the "host cluster." The host cluster will be responsible for deploying and managing the KubeFed control plane, which in turn will oversee the federation of other clusters. For instance, in this scenario, cluster1 has been chosen as the host cluster. This means that cluster1 will serve as the central hub for managing the other clusters in the federation, allowing for greater scalability and flexibility in the deployment and management of applications across multiple cloud environments.

Set the KUBECONFIG environment variable to the kubeconfig file of the host cluster:

```
export KUBECONFIG=cluster1-kubeconfig.yaml
```

Deploy the KubeFed control plane in the host cluster:

```
kubectl kubefed init my-federation --host-cluster-context=cluster1 --image=quay.io/kubernetes-multicluster/kubefed:v0.8.1 --dns-provider="google-clouddns" --dns-zone-name="example.com." --etcd-persistent-storage=false
```

Replace --dns-provider, --dns-zone-name, and --image with the appropriate values for your environment. For a production setup, you may want to use --etcd-persistent-storage=true to store etcd data persistently.

Join Clusters to the Federation

To federate the Kubernetes clusters, deploy the KubeFed control plane and utilize the kubefedctl tool to join the clusters to the federation. This will enable efficient management of the clusters as a single entity, allowing for the deployment and management of applications across multiple clusters simultaneously.

Join cluster1 (host cluster) to the federation:

```
kubefedctl join cluster1 --cluster-context=cluster1
--host-cluster-context=cluster1
```

Join cluster2 to the federation:

```
kubefedctl join cluster2 --cluster-context=cluster2 --host-cluster-
context=cluster1
```

Verify Clusters are Federated

You can verify that the clusters are federated by checking the KubeFedCluster resources in the host cluster:

```
kubectl get kubefedclusters -n kube-federation-system
```

You should see both cluster1 and cluster2 listed as federated clusters.

Deploy Federated Application

Now that your clusters are federated, you can deploy an application to all federated clusters. Create a FederatedDeployment and FederatedService to deploy the application.

For example, create a federated-nginx.yaml file with the following contents:

```
apiVersion: types.kubefed.io/v1beta1
kind: FederatedDeployment
```

```yaml
metadata:
  name: nginx
spec:
  template:
    metadata:
      labels:
        app: nginx
    spec:
      replicas: 2
      selector:
        matchLabels:
          app: nginx
      template:
        metadata:
          labels:
            app: nginx
        spec:
          containers:
          - name: nginx
            image: nginx:1.14.2
            ports:
            - containerPort: 80
apiVersion: types.kubefed.io/v1beta1
kind: FederatedService
metadata:
  name: nginx
spec:
  template:
    spec:
      selector:
        app: nginx
      ports:
```

- name: http
port: 80
targetPort: 80

Apply the `FederatedDeployment` and `FederatedService` to the federated clusters:

kubectl apply -f federated-nginx.yaml

This will deploy the Nginx application in both cluster1 and cluster2.

Verify the Application Deployment

To verify that the application is running in both clusters, switch the KUBECONFIG environment variable to each cluster's kubeconfig file and check the resources.

For cluster1

export KUBECONFIG=cluster1-kubeconfig.yaml
kubectl get deployments,svc

For cluster2

export KUBECONFIG=cluster2-kubeconfig.yaml
kubectl get deployments,svc

You should see the Nginx deployment and service running in both clusters.

Clean Up

To remove the federation, you can delete the KubeFed namespace and the kubefedclusters resources.

Delete the namespace:

kubectl delete ns kube-federation-system

Delete the kubefedclusters resources:

```
kubectl delete kubefedclusters -A
```

And, you've successfully set up and configured Kubernetes multi-cluster federation using KubeFed. You can now manage resources across multiple Kubernetes clusters, making it easier to deploy and maintain applications in a multi-cluster environment. Keep in mind that KubeFed is still a relatively young project, and its functionality may continue to evolve over time. Be sure to stay up-to-date with the latest developments and best practices for managing federated Kubernetes clusters.

Deploying Applications Across Clusters

Once you have set up a multi-cluster environment using Kubernetes Federation (KubeFed), you can deploy applications across the federated clusters. In this section, we'll walk through the process of deploying a sample application to multiple clusters using KubeFed.

Create the Federated Resources

To deploy an application across multiple federated clusters, you need to create federated resource definitions, such as FederatedDeployment and FederatedService. These resources allow you to synchronize the application's deployment and service across all federated clusters.

Create a file called federated-app.yaml with the following contents:

```yaml
apiVersion: types.kubefed.io/v1beta1
kind: FederatedDeployment
metadata:
  name: my-app
spec:
  template:
    metadata:
      labels:
        app: my-app
    spec:
```

```yaml
      replicas: 2
      selector:
       matchLabels:
        app: my-app
      template:
       metadata:
        labels:
         app: my-app
       spec:
        containers:
        - name: my-app
          image: my-app-image:latest
          ports:
          - containerPort: 80
---
apiVersion: types.kubefed.io/v1beta1
kind: FederatedService
metadata:
 name: my-app
spec:
 template:
  spec:
   selector:
    app: my-app
   ports:
    - name: http
      port: 80
      targetPort: 80
```

Replace my-app-image:latest with the appropriate Docker image for your application.

Apply the Federated Resources

With the federated-app.yaml file ready, apply it to the federated clusters using kubectl:

```
kubectl apply -f federated-app.yaml
```

This command will create a FederatedDeployment and a FederatedService for your application, which will automatically synchronize the deployment and service to all the federated clusters.

Verify the Application Deployment

To verify that the application is running in all the federated clusters, you can use kubectl to check the resources in each cluster. Make sure to switch the KUBECONFIG environment variable to each cluster's kubeconfig file before running the commands.

For example, assuming you have two clusters named cluster1 and cluster2:

For cluster1

```
export KUBECONFIG=cluster1-kubeconfig.yaml
kubectl get deployments,svc
```

For cluster2

```
export KUBECONFIG=cluster2-kubeconfig.yaml
kubectl get deployments,svc
```

You should see the deployment and service running in both clusters.

Access the Application

To access the application running in each cluster, you can use the cluster's load balancer or ingress controller. Keep in mind that the specific method for accessing your application may vary depending on your cluster's configuration and cloud provider.

If you have a FederatedIngress set up for your application, you can use it to distribute traffic between the federated clusters. Otherwise, you can access the application through each cluster's load balancer or ingress controller individually.

With this, you have deployed an application across multiple federated Kubernetes clusters using KubeFed. This approach allows you to manage your application's deployment and service across all clusters simultaneously, simplifying the process of deploying and maintaining applications in a multi-cluster environment.

Cluster-aware Service Routing

Cluster-aware service routing is a mechanism that enables service requests to be intelligently distributed among multiple Kubernetes clusters based on factors like cluster load, service availability, and the geographic location of the requester. This approach ensures that the service requests are handled by the most appropriate cluster, resulting in improved application performance, resilience, and efficient resource utilization.

In a multi-cluster environment, cluster-aware service routing is essential to provide an optimal user experience and distribute the workload evenly across clusters. Some key advantages of cluster-aware service routing include:

- Load balancing: Cluster-aware service routing can distribute the load across multiple clusters, preventing a single cluster from being overwhelmed with requests while others remain underutilized.
- High availability: By routing requests to the most suitable cluster, cluster-aware service routing ensures the availability of the requested service even if a particular cluster experiences an outage or has limited resources.
- Latency reduction: Cluster-aware service routing can direct requests to the cluster closest to the requester, minimizing network latency and improving the user experience.
- Cost optimization: By balancing the load across clusters, cluster-aware service routing helps organizations optimize their cloud infrastructure costs.

In a multi-cluster Kubernetes environment, it's essential to implement cluster-aware service routing to distribute traffic across multiple clusters effectively. There are several ways to achieve this, and we will discuss some of the most popular methods below.

One way to implement cluster-aware service routing is by using a global load balancer. This method involves setting up an external DNS service that routes requests to the most appropriate cluster based on factors such as geographic location, cluster load, and health status. Major cloud providers like AWS, GCP, and Azure offer global load balancing solutions that can be integrated with multi-cluster Kubernetes environments. With this method, you can ensure that incoming traffic is always directed to the cluster that can best handle it, resulting in improved performance and reliability.

Another way to implement cluster-aware service routing is through Federated Ingress. This approach involves using FederatedIngress to manage ingress resources across federated clusters, allowing you to define ingress rules that span multiple clusters. This enables cluster-aware service routing, and the actual implementation may vary depending on the ingress controller used and any additional configuration required to integrate with a global load balancer or external DNS service. This approach is beneficial as it enables you to centralize the management of ingress resources, making it easier to manage multiple clusters.

A third method for implementing cluster-aware service routing is through a service mesh like Istio, Linkerd, or Consul. Service meshes provide advanced routing, load balancing, and security features across multiple clusters, offering a unified platform for managing and securing inter-service communication. With service mesh solutions, you can define routing rules that take into consideration factors such as cluster load, latency, and health status to route requests to the most appropriate cluster. This method is highly beneficial as it provides granular control over traffic routing, making it easier to manage complex multi-cluster environments.

Cluster-aware service routing is a crucial aspect of multi-cluster Kubernetes environments, as it helps distribute the workload across clusters and improve the overall performance and resilience of the deployed services. Various tools and technologies can be employed to implement cluster-aware service routing, including global load balancers, federated ingress, and service meshes.

MultiCluster Resource Management

Kubernetes Federation (KubeFed) allows you to manage resources across multiple Kubernetes clusters. With KubeFed, you can synchronize the deployment and configuration of resources, making it easier to maintain applications in multi-cluster environments. In this section, we'll walk through the process of managing resources across multiple clusters using KubeFed.

Deploy KubeFed

Before you can manage resources with KubeFed, you need to set up a KubeFed control plane in your host cluster. We've already covered the deployment and configuration of KubeFed in a previous section, so make sure you have a KubeFed control plane deployed and your clusters joined to the federation.

Create Federated Resources

To manage resources across multiple federated clusters, you need to create federated resource definitions. These resources allow you to synchronize the deployment and configuration of the desired Kubernetes resources across all federated clusters.

For example, to create a federated ConfigMap, you would create a FederatedConfigMap resource like this:

```
apiVersion: types.kubefed.io/v1beta1
kind: FederatedConfigMap
metadata:
  name: my-config
spec:
  template:
    data:
      my-key: my-value
```

Apply the Federated Resources

With the federated resource definition file ready, apply it to the federated clusters using kubectl:

```
kubectl apply -f federated-configmap.yaml
```

This command will create a FederatedConfigMap for your configuration, which will automatically synchronize the ConfigMap to all the federated clusters.

Verify the Resource Synchronization

To verify that the resource is synchronized across all the federated clusters, you can use kubectl to check the resource in each cluster. Make sure to switch the KUBECONFIG environment variable to each cluster's kubeconfig file before running the commands.

For example, assuming you have two clusters named cluster1 and cluster2:

For cluster1

```
export KUBECONFIG=cluster1-kubeconfig.yaml
kubectl get configmap my-config
```

```
export KUBECONFIG=cluster2-kubeconfig.yaml
kubectl get configmap my-config
```

You should see the ConfigMap present in both clusters.

Manage Resources Across Clusters

With KubeFed, you can manage various types of Kubernetes resources across multiple clusters. Some common federated resources include:
- FederatedDeployment
- FederatedService
- FederatedConfigMap
- FederatedSecret
- FederatedIngress
- FederatedNamespace

To manage these resources, you simply need to create a federated resource definition for the desired Kubernetes resource type and apply it using kubectl. KubeFed will then synchronize the resource across all federated clusters.

Remember that KubeFed is particularly useful for managing resources that need to be consistent across multiple clusters. For resources that require cluster-specific configurations, you might need to use other tools or techniques, such as Helm or Kustomize.

Overall, KubeFed simplifies multi-cluster resource management by enabling you to synchronize the deployment and configuration of resources across federated clusters. With KubeFed, you can maintain a consistent state for your applications and resources in multi-cluster environments, making it easier to deploy and manage applications at scale.

Monitoring and Logging in MultiCluster Environments

Monitoring and logging in a multi-cluster environment with KubeFed can be achieved by leveraging centralized monitoring and logging tools. In this section, we'll cover the setup and configuration of two popular tools for multi-cluster monitoring and logging: Prometheus and Grafana for monitoring, and Elasticsearch, Fluentd, and Kibana (EFK stack) for logging.

Monitoring with Prometheus and Grafana

Prometheus is a popular open-source monitoring and alerting toolkit, while Grafana is an open-source platform for data visualization, monitoring, and analysis. Together, they provide a powerful solution for monitoring Kubernetes clusters.

Deploy Prometheus and Grafana in a central cluster

Choose one of your Kubernetes clusters to act as the central monitoring cluster. You can deploy Prometheus and Grafana using their respective Helm charts or Kubernetes manifests. Make sure to configure Prometheus to scrape metrics from all your federated clusters.

Configure Prometheus to scrape metrics from all clusters

To configure Prometheus to scrape metrics from all your federated clusters, you'll need to create a prometheus.yml configuration file that includes the endpoints for each cluster's kube-apiserver and kubelet components.

Example prometheus.yml configuration:

```
scrape_configs:
  - job_name: 'federated-kubernetes'
    metrics_path: /metrics
    static_configs:
      - targets: ['cluster1-kube-apiserver:6443', 'cluster2-kube-apiserver:6443']
        labels:
          group: 'kube-apiserver'
      - targets: ['cluster1-kubelet:10250', 'cluster2-kubelet:10250']
        labels:
          group: 'kubelet'
```

Replace the targets values with the correct endpoints for your clusters. Apply the configuration to your Prometheus deployment.

Set up Grafana dashboards for multi-cluster monitoring

Once you have Prometheus scraping metrics from all your federated clusters, you can create

Grafana dashboards to visualize the data. Import or create Grafana dashboards that display the desired metrics for each cluster. You can use variables and filters to enable switching between clusters within a single dashboard.

Logging with Elasticsearch, Fluentd, and Kibana (EFK stack)

Elasticsearch, Fluentd, and Kibana form a popular open-source stack for log management and analysis. The EFK stack can be used to aggregate logs from multiple Kubernetes clusters into a centralized logging platform.

Deploy Elasticsearch and Kibana in a central cluster

Choose one of your Kubernetes clusters to act as the central logging cluster. Deploy Elasticsearch and Kibana using their respective Helm charts or Kubernetes manifests.

Deploy Fluentd as a DaemonSet on each federated cluster

Fluentd will be used to collect and forward logs from each cluster to the central Elasticsearch cluster. Deploy Fluentd as a DaemonSet on each of your federated clusters, ensuring that it runs on every node.

Configure Fluentd to forward logs to Elasticsearch

Create a Fluentd configuration file (fluentd-configmap.yaml) that specifies the Elasticsearch endpoint and the desired log sources. Example configuration:

```yaml
apiVersion: v1
kind: ConfigMap
metadata:
  name: fluentd-config
data:
  fluent.conf: |
    <source>
      @type tail
      path /var/log/containers/*.log
      pos_file /var/log/fluentd-containers.log.pos
      tag kubernetes.*
      format json
```

```
    read_from_head true
  </source>
  <match kubernetes.*>
   @type elasticsearch
   host <elasticsearch-service-name>
   port 9200
   logstash_format true
   logstash_prefix fluentd
   include_tag_key true
   type_name container_logs
   <buffer>
    flush_mode interval
    flush_interval 10s
    chunk_limit_size 2M
    queue_limit_length 8
   </buffer>
  </match>
```

Replace `<elasticsearch-service-name>` with the appropriate service name or endpoint for your central Elasticsearch cluster.

Apply the Fluentd configuration to each federated cluster
Apply the `fluentd-configmap.yaml` configuration file to each of your federated clusters using `kubectl`:

```
kubectl apply -f fluentd-configmap.yaml
```

Create Kibana dashboards for multi-cluster log analysis
With Fluentd forwarding logs from all your federated clusters to Elasticsearch, you can create Kibana dashboards to analyze and visualize the log data. You can use filters and queries to analyze logs from specific clusters or across all clusters.

Overall, monitoring and logging in a multi-cluster KubeFed environment can be achieved by using centralized monitoring and logging tools like Prometheus, Grafana, Elasticsearch,

Fluentd, and Kibana. By configuring these tools to collect and visualize data from all federated clusters, you can effectively manage and analyze your multi-cluster environment.

Summary

In this discussion, we covered various aspects of multi-cluster management in Kubernetes environments, including multi-cloud, cross-cluster networking, service discovery, load balancing, monitoring, and logging.

We introduced Submariner, a tool that enables secure network connectivity between Kubernetes clusters across different networks or clouds. We discussed the installation and configuration process for Submariner in a multi-cloud setup with AWS and GCP, as well as implementing cross-cluster networking and service discovery using it.

We also explored multi-cluster federation using Kubernetes Federation (KubeFed) and how it simplifies managing resources across multiple Kubernetes clusters by synchronizing deployments and configurations. We discussed setting up and configuring multi-cluster federation, deploying applications across federated clusters, and implementing cluster-aware service routing using global load balancers, federated ingress, or service mesh solutions.

Furthermore, we covered monitoring and logging in multi-cluster environments, utilizing centralized monitoring and logging tools like Prometheus, Grafana, Elasticsearch, Fluentd, and Kibana. We outlined the steps to configure these tools to collect and visualize data from all federated clusters, enabling effective management and analysis of multi-cluster environments.

Overall, managing a multi-cluster Kubernetes environment requires a combination of tools and techniques to ensure consistent application deployment, efficient resource utilization, and robust monitoring and logging. By leveraging tools like Submariner, KubeFed, and centralized monitoring/logging solutions, organizations can streamline their multi-cluster management processes and maintain optimal performance and resilience in their Kubernetes deployments.

CHAPTER 7: MULTI-CLOUD CI/CD PIPELINES

Understanding CI/CD in Multi-cloud Environments

Continuous Integration and Continuous Deployment (CI/CD) is a critical aspect of modern application development, and Kubernetes has become a popular platform to implement it. With the emergence of multi-cloud environments, CI/CD has evolved to accommodate the complexity and challenges of these new architectures. Multi-cloud CI/CD is different from conventional CI/CD in several ways. First, it requires a robust and reliable infrastructure that can span multiple cloud providers and data centers. This infrastructure must be designed to handle the unique challenges of multi-cloud environments, such as data synchronization, network latency, and security. Second, it requires a unified approach to configuration management, which can ensure consistency and compliance across all environments. This approach must be flexible enough to support different cloud providers and configurations while maintaining a centralized source of truth. Finally, it requires a comprehensive monitoring and analytics system, which can provide real-time visibility into the performance and health of the application across all environments.

Multi-cloud vs. Conventional CI/CD

Multi-cloud CI/CD aims to enable the continuous integration and deployment of applications across multiple cloud providers, whereas conventional CI/CD is designed for single-cloud or on-premises environments. Below are some key differences:

- Multi-cloud environments add complexity by involving multiple cloud providers with different APIs, services, and infrastructure components.
- Network latency and data transfer costs are critical factors in multi-cloud CI/CD, as applications may be distributed across different regions and cloud providers.
- Multi-cloud CI/CD requires enhanced security measures to protect sensitive data and maintain compliance with each cloud provider's regulations.
- The need for multi-cloud management tools and platforms has increased, requiring seamless integration with CI/CD pipelines.

Multi-cloud CI/CD in Kubernetes

Kubernetes provides a consistent and extensible platform for deploying, scaling, and managing containerized applications. By using Kubernetes, multi-cloud CI/CD can be implemented more efficiently. Below is how it is implemented:

Kubernetes Federation (KubeFed)

KubeFed enables you to manage multiple Kubernetes clusters, simplifying the deployment, management, and scaling of applications across multiple cloud providers. It allows you to synchronize resources across clusters, ensuring that your CI/CD pipelines run seamlessly in multi-cloud environments.

Virtual Kubelet

Virtual Kubelet extends Kubernetes to non-Kubernetes platforms, making it possible to deploy containers in environments that don't natively support Kubernetes. This makes it easier to implement CI/CD pipelines that span multiple cloud providers, as you can deploy applications in the same way regardless of the underlying infrastructure.

Submariner

Submariner is a Kubernetes multi-cluster networking solution that enables secure communication between clusters across different cloud providers. It simplifies CI/CD pipelines by providing a unified network layer for your applications, allowing you to deploy and manage them consistently across multiple cloud providers.

Multi-cloud CI/CD Tools and Strategies

Several tools and strategies can help you implement multi-cloud CI/CD in your Kubernetes environment:

GitOps

GitOps is a CI/CD strategy where Git is used as the single source of truth for infrastructure and application deployment. It enables you to manage multi-cloud deployments with ease by treating infrastructure and application code as any other code, allowing you to use the same version control and CI/CD processes.

Helm

Helm is a package manager for Kubernetes, which can help you manage your application deployments across multiple clusters and cloud providers. Helm charts define, install, and upgrade Kubernetes applications, making it easy to manage and deploy applications consistently across different environments.

Argo CD

Argo CD is a declarative, GitOps-based continuous delivery tool for Kubernetes. It helps you manage and synchronize application deployment across multiple clusters, allowing you to implement multi-cloud CI/CD pipelines with ease.

Crossplane

Crossplane is an open-source infrastructure management platform that allows you to manage your cloud resources using Kubernetes APIs. It enables you to provision, manage, and deploy applications across multiple cloud providers, simplifying multi-cloud CI/CD.

Best Practices for Multi-cloud CI/CD in Kubernetes

Below are some best practices to help you implement multi-cloud CI/CD in Kubernetes:

- Use a centralized version control system like Git to manage your infrastructure and application code, ensuring version control and consistency across multiple cloud providers.
- Use a CI/CD pipeline that integrates with Kubernetes, ensuring that you can deploy applications consistently across multiple clusters and cloud providers.
- Use Kubernetes Federation (KubeFed) to manage multiple Kubernetes clusters across different cloud providers, enabling you to deploy and manage applications consistently.
- Use Virtual Kubelet to extend Kubernetes to non-Kubernetes platforms, making it possible to deploy containers in environments that don't natively support Kubernetes.
- Use Submariner to provide a unified network layer for your applications, enabling secure communication between clusters across different cloud providers.
- Use tools like Helm, Argo CD, and Crossplane to manage your application deployments across multiple clusters and cloud providers, simplifying the process of multi-cloud CI/CD.
- Monitor your multi-cloud CI/CD pipelines closely, ensuring that you can identify and fix issues quickly and efficiently.

Multi-cloud environments have become increasingly popular in recent years, and Kubernetes has emerged as a key platform for implementing multi-cloud CI/CD. By using tools like Kubernetes Federation, Virtual Kubelet, and Submariner, and strategies like GitOps and Helm, you can simplify the process of deploying and managing applications across multiple cloud providers. Best practices like using version control, monitoring closely, and integrating with Kubernetes can help you ensure consistency and efficiency in your multi-cloud CI/CD pipelines.

Setting up Multi-cloud CI/CD Pipelines with Jenkins

Establishing a multi-cloud Continuous Integration/Continuous Deployment (CI/CD) pipeline through Kubernetes Federation (KubeFed), Virtual Kubelet, and Jenkins is a robust method of streamlining the deployment process for applications across several cloud providers. This approach enables organizations to automate and orchestrate deployments effectively, ensuring the applications are available to end-users across multiple cloud platforms. By utilizing KubeFed and Virtual Kubelet, Kubernetes can orchestrate resources across multiple clusters and cloud providers, simplifying the deployment process. Additionally, Jenkins can be integrated to automate the entire CI/CD pipeline, ensuring smooth and efficient application delivery.

Below are the steps to set it up:

Set up Kubernetes Clusters

Before setting up the CI/CD pipeline, ensure that you have created Kubernetes clusters on both AWS and GCP. You can use any tool like kops, Kubespray, or even managed Kubernetes services like EKS and GKE.

Install Jenkins

Next, you need to install Jenkins on a machine that has access to both Kubernetes clusters. You can use any method to install Jenkins, but I would recommend using the official Jenkins Helm chart to simplify the installation process.

To install Jenkins using Helm, run the following commands:

```
helm repo add jenkins https://charts.jenkins.io
helm repo update
helm install jenkins jenkins/jenkins --namespace jenkins --set
serviceType=LoadBalancer --set agent.enabled=true
```

This command installs Jenkins on the Kubernetes cluster in the jenkins namespace as a LoadBalancer service. The agent.enabled=true flag is used to enable Kubernetes agent pods to run Jenkins builds.

Configure Jenkins

After installing Jenkins, you need to configure it to use Kubernetes Federation and Virtual Kubelet to deploy applications across AWS and GCP.

First, install the Kubernetes plugin on Jenkins to allow Jenkins to communicate with the Kubernetes clusters. You can install the Kubernetes plugin from the Jenkins plugin manager.

Next, configure the Kubernetes plugin to use the kubeconfig files for both AWS and GCP clusters. You can use the following command to extract the kubeconfig files from the Kubernetes clusters:

```
kubectl config view --flatten > kubeconfig.yaml
```

This command extracts the Kubernetes configuration into a file named kubeconfig.yaml. You need to run this command on both AWS and GCP clusters and save the kubeconfig.yaml files.

Once you have the kubeconfig.yaml files, add them to Jenkins as Kubernetes credentials. To do this, navigate to "Jenkins > Credentials > System > Global credentials (unrestricted)" and click "Add Credentials." Choose "Kubernetes configuration (kubeconfig)" from the credentials type dropdown, and add the path to the kubeconfig.yaml files.

Create Jenkins Pipeline

Finally, create a Jenkins pipeline that builds and deploys your application across AWS and GCP using Kubernetes Federation and Virtual Kubelet. Below is an example pipeline:

```
pipeline {
  agent {
    kubernetes {
      label 'virtual-kubelet'
      cloud 'virtual-kubelet'
      containerTemplate {
        name 'virtual-kubelet'
        image 'virtual-kubelet:latest'
        ttyEnabled true
        command 'cat'
      }
    }
  }
```

```groovy
stages {
    stage('Build') {
        steps {
            sh 'make build'
        }
    }


    stage('Deploy') {
        steps {
            kubefedctl join cluster aws --cluster-context aws --host-cluster-
context host --v=2
            kubefedctl join cluster gcp --cluster-context gcp --host-cluster-context
host --v=2


            kubectl config use-context host

            kubectl create ns myapp

            kubectl apply -f kubernetes/service.yaml
            kubectl apply -f kubernetes/deployment.yaml

            kubectl config use-context aws

            kubectl create ns myapp

            kubectl apply -f kubernetes/service.yaml
            kubectl apply -f kubernetes/deployment.yaml

            kubectl config use-context gcp

            kubectl create ns myapp
```

```
        kubectl apply -f kubernetes/service.yaml
        kubectl apply -f kubernetes/deployment.yaml

        kubectl config use-context host
    }
  }
 }
}
```

This pipeline consists of two stages: `Build` and `Deploy`. The `Build` stage is responsible for building your application, while the `Deploy` stage deploys it across the Kubernetes clusters on AWS and GCP using Kubernetes Federation and Virtual Kubelet.

In the `Deploy` stage, we first use `kubefedctl` to join the AWS and GCP clusters to the Kubernetes Federation cluster. The `--cluster-context` flag specifies the Kubernetes context of the remote cluster, while the `--host-cluster-context` flag specifies the Kubernetes context of the host cluster.

Next, we switch to the Kubernetes Federation context and create a namespace for our application. We then deploy the service and deployment manifests to the Kubernetes Federation cluster, which distributes them to the AWS and GCP clusters via Virtual Kubelet.

Finally, we switch to the AWS and GCP cluster contexts and repeat the deployment process for each cluster.

You now have a multi-cloud CI/CD pipeline using Kubernetes Federation, Virtual Kubelet, and Jenkins that deploys applications across AWS and GCP.

Building and Deploying Applications across Clusters

After successfully setting up a multi-cloud CI/CD pipeline with Kubernetes Federation and Jenkins, you can efficiently build and deploy applications across multiple Kubernetes clusters. The use of Kubernetes Federation provides a centralized control plane for managing the multiple clusters, while Jenkins automates the build and deployment process.

With this approach, you can ensure seamless deployment of applications on different cloud providers, which enhances the scalability and resilience of your infrastructure.

Below is how it is executed:

Create Application Code

First, create your application code and package it as a container image using a Dockerfile. The Dockerfile should define the dependencies and environment needed to run your application.

Push Container Image to Container Registry

Next, push the container image to a container registry such as Docker Hub or Amazon ECR. This will make the container image available for deployment across multiple Kubernetes clusters.

Define Kubernetes Manifests

Next, define the Kubernetes manifests that describe your application. These manifests should include a Deployment object that defines the number of replicas of your application, and a Service object that defines how your application is accessed.

For example, Below is a sample Kubernetes manifest for a simple Flask application:

```
apiVersion: apps/v1
kind: Deployment
metadata:
  name: myapp
spec:
  replicas: 3
  selector:
    matchLabels:
      app: myapp
  template:
    metadata:
      labels:
        app: myapp
```

```yaml
spec:
  containers:
  - name: myapp
    image: <container-registry>/<image-name>:<tag>
    ports:
    - containerPort: 5000
---
apiVersion: v1
kind: Service
metadata:
  name: myapp
spec:
  selector:
    app: myapp
  ports:
  - name: http
    port: 80
    targetPort: 5000
  type: LoadBalancer
```

Deploy the application using Jenkins

Finally, deploy your application to multiple Kubernetes clusters using the Jenkins pipeline you created earlier. You can trigger the pipeline manually, or you can set up a webhook to automatically trigger the pipeline when new code is pushed to your repository.

When you trigger the pipeline, Jenkins will build your application code, package it as a container image, and deploy it to the Kubernetes clusters using Kubernetes Federation and Virtual Kubelet.

Once the deployment is complete, you can access your application by connecting to the LoadBalancer service that was created in the Kubernetes manifest. You have now successfully built and deployed your application across multiple Kubernetes clusters using Kubernetes Federation, Virtual Kubelet, and Jenkins.

Managing Configuration and Secrets

Managing configurations and secrets across multiple Kubernetes clusters can be a daunting task. However, using Kubernetes ConfigMaps and Secrets can help simplify this process. ConfigMaps store configuration data as key-value pairs, which can be used to configure containers and Kubernetes objects. Secrets, on the other hand, store sensitive information like passwords and API keys in an encrypted format. By using these Kubernetes features, administrators can manage configurations and secrets consistently across multiple clusters, reducing the risk of errors and misconfigurations.

Below is how to use them:

Define ConfigMaps and Secrets

First, define your ConfigMaps and Secrets that contain the configuration and secrets for your application. For example, you might define a ConfigMap that contains environment variables, and a Secret that contains a database password.

Below is an example of how to define a ConfigMap and Secret in Kubernetes:

```yaml
apiVersion: v1
kind: ConfigMap
metadata:
  name: myapp-config
data:
  MYAPP_ENV: "production"
  MYAPP_DEBUG: "false"
---
apiVersion: v1
kind: Secret
metadata:
  name: myapp-secret
type: Opaque
data:
  DB_PASSWORD: <base64-encoded-password>
```

Deploy your ConfigMaps and Secrets to Kubernetes Federation

Next, deploy your ConfigMaps and Secrets to the Kubernetes Federation cluster using kubectl apply. You can define the ConfigMaps and Secrets in the same YAML file as your application manifests, or in a separate YAML file.

For example, Below is how to deploy the ConfigMap and Secret we defined earlier:

```
kubectl apply -f myapp-config.yaml
kubectl apply -f myapp-secret.yaml
```

Reference your ConfigMaps and Secrets in your application manifests
After deploying your ConfigMaps and Secrets, reference them in your application manifests using environment variables or volume mounts.

For example, Below is how to reference the ConfigMap and Secret we defined earlier in our deployment manifest:

```
apiVersion: apps/v1
kind: Deployment
metadata:
 name: myapp
spec:
 replicas: 3
 selector:
   matchLabels:
     app: myapp
 template:
   metadata:
     labels:
       app: myapp
   spec:
     containers:
     - name: myapp
```

```yaml
image: <container-registry>/<image-name>:<tag>
env:
- name: MYAPP_ENV
  valueFrom:
   configMapKeyRef:
    name: myapp-config
    key: MYAPP_ENV
- name: MYAPP_DEBUG
  valueFrom:
   configMapKeyRef:
    name: myapp-config
    key: MYAPP_DEBUG
- name: DB_PASSWORD
  valueFrom:
   secretKeyRef:
    name: myapp-secret
    key: DB_PASSWORD
```

In the above demonstrated example, we reference the MYAPP_ENV and MYAPP_DEBUG environment variables from the myapp-config ConfigMap, and the DB_PASSWORD environment variable from the myapp-secret Secret.

Deploy Application to Multiple Kubernetes Clusters

Finally, deploy your application to multiple Kubernetes clusters using the Jenkins pipeline you created earlier. When the pipeline deploys your application, it will also deploy the ConfigMaps and Secrets to the Kubernetes Federation cluster, and distribute them to the AWS and GCP clusters via Virtual Kubelet.

Testing in Multi-cloud CI/CD

Testing in a multi-cloud CI/CD environment is crucial for ensuring the successful deployment and maintenance of applications. This involves setting up a multi-cloud Kubernetes cluster, configuring AWS and GCP credentials, and using tools like kubectl to manage deployments. Testing should be conducted at every stage of the development process, from unit testing to integration testing and end-to-end testing. Additionally, various types of testing, such as load testing, security testing, and performance testing, should be conducted to ensure the application functions effectively across multiple cloud environments. Effective testing in a multi-cloud CI/CD environment can help identify and resolve issues before they impact users, leading to a more reliable and efficient application.

Below are the steps:

Create Application Code

First, create your application code and package it as a container image using a Dockerfile. The Dockerfile should define the dependencies and environment needed to run your application.

Push Container Image to Container Registry

Next, push the container image to a container registry such as Docker Hub, Amazon ECR, or Google Container Registry. This will make the container image available for deployment across multiple Kubernetes clusters.

Define Kubernetes Manifests

Next, define the Kubernetes manifests that describe your application. These manifests should include a Deployment object that defines the number of replicas of your application, and a Service object that defines how your application is accessed.

For example, Below is a sample Kubernetes manifest for a simple Flask application:

```
apiVersion: apps/v1
kind: Deployment
metadata:
  name: myapp
spec:
  replicas: 3
  selector:
    matchLabels:
      app: myapp
  template:
    metadata:
```

```yaml
    labels:
      app: myapp
  spec:
    containers:
    - name: myapp
      image: <container-registry>/<image-name>:<tag>
      ports:
      - containerPort: 5000
---
apiVersion: v1
kind: Service
metadata:
  name: myapp
spec:
  selector:
    app: myapp
  ports:
  - name: http
    port: 80
    targetPort: 5000
  type: LoadBalancer
```

Deploy Application using Jenkins

Now, let us create a Jenkins pipeline to deploy our application to multiple Kubernetes clusters on AWS and GCP. Below is a sample Jenkinsfile that you can use as a starting point:

```groovy
pipeline {
  agent any
  stages {
    stage('Build') {
      steps {
```

```
                sh 'docker build -t <container-registry>/<image-name>:<tag> .'
                sh 'docker push <container-registry>/<image-name>:<tag>'
            }
        }
        stage('Deploy') {
            steps {
                sh 'kubefedctl join aws --cluster-context=aws'
                sh 'kubefedctl join gcp --cluster-context=gcp'
                sh 'kubectl config use-context federation'
                sh 'kubectl create namespace myapp'
                sh 'kubectl apply -f kubernetes/service.yaml'
                sh 'kubectl apply -f kubernetes/deployment.yaml'
                sh 'kubectl config use-context aws'
                sh 'kubectl create namespace myapp'
                sh 'kubectl apply -f kubernetes/service.yaml'
                sh 'kubectl apply -f kubernetes/deployment.yaml'
                sh 'kubectl config use-context gcp'
                sh 'kubectl create namespace myapp'
                sh 'kubectl apply -f kubernetes/service.yaml'
                sh 'kubectl apply -f kubernetes/deployment.yaml'
            }
        }
    }
}
```

This pipeline consists of two stages: Build and Deploy. The Build stage is responsible for building your application, while the Deploy stage deploys it across the Kubernetes clusters on AWS and GCP using Kubernetes Federation.

In the Deploy stage, we first use kubefedctl to join the AWS and GCP clusters to the Kubernetes Federation cluster. The --cluster-context flag specifies the Kubernetes context of the remote cluster.

Next, we switch to the Kubernetes Federation context and create a namespace for our application. We then deploy the service and deployment manifests to the Kubernetes Federation cluster, which distributes them to the AWS and GCP clusters using Kubernetes Federation and Virtual Kubelet.

Finally, we switch to each of the AWS and GCP cluster contexts and deploy the service and deployment manifests to each cluster separately.

Add Unit and Integration Tests to Pipeline

To add unit and integration tests to your pipeline, you can create a new stage in your Jenkinsfile that runs your tests. Below is an example:

```
stage('Test') {
    steps {
        sh 'kubefedctl join aws --cluster-context=aws'
        sh 'kubefedctl join gcp --cluster-context=gcp'
        sh 'kubectl config use-context federation'
        sh 'helm install --name myapp-test kubernetes/charts/myapp --set environment=test'
        sh 'kubectl config use-context aws'
        sh 'helm install --name myapp-test kubernetes/charts/myapp --set environment=test'
        sh 'kubectl config use-context gcp'
        sh 'helm install --name myapp-test kubernetes/charts/myapp --set environment=test'
    }
}
```

In this stage, we use helm to install a test version of our application to each Kubernetes cluster. We set the environment value to test to indicate that this is a test deployment.

Once the test deployment is complete, you can run your unit and integration tests against the test version of your application.

Monitor the Pipeline

Finally, monitor the pipeline to ensure that it is running smoothly and catching any issues that might arise. Use monitoring tools to track the performance and stability of your application across all the Kubernetes clusters.

For example, you might use a tool like Prometheus to monitor your application's performance, or a tool like ELK stack to monitor your application's logs.

By following these steps, you can set up a multi-cloud CI/CD pipeline using Kubernetes, Jenkins, and AWS and GCP clusters, and add unit and integration testing to your pipeline to ensure that your application is thoroughly tested in a multi-cloud environment.

Multi-cloud CI/CD Pipeline Monitoring

Let us walk through a practical demonstration of monitoring a multi-cloud CI/CD pipeline using Prometheus in a step-by-step manner. Below are the steps:

Define Metrics to Monitor

First, define the metrics that you want to monitor for your application. These might include metrics such as CPU usage, memory usage, and network traffic.

You can instrument your application to expose these metrics using tools like Prometheus client libraries.

Configure Prometheus to Scrape Metrics

Next, configure Prometheus to scrape the metrics from your application. This involves adding a ServiceMonitor object to your Kubernetes cluster that specifies the endpoint where your application exposes the metrics.

Below is an example ServiceMonitor object:

```
apiVersion: monitoring.coreos.com/v1
kind: ServiceMonitor
metadata:
  name: myapp-monitor
spec:
  selector:
    matchLabels:
      app: myapp
```

```
endpoints:
- port: metrics
```

In the above demonstrated example, we define a ServiceMonitor object named myapp-monitor that selects pods with the app=myapp label. We also specify an endpoint named metrics where our application exposes its metrics.

Configure Grafana to Visualize the Metrics

Next, configure Grafana to visualize the metrics collected by Prometheus. This involves adding a Prometheus data source to Grafana and creating dashboards that display the metrics in a meaningful way.

You can use the Grafana UI to create and configure your dashboards, or you can import pre-built dashboards from the Grafana dashboard repository.

Monitor the Pipeline

Finally, monitor the pipeline to ensure that it is running smoothly and catching any issues that might arise. Use the metrics collected by Prometheus and displayed in Grafana to track the performance and stability of your application across all the Kubernetes clusters.

For example, you might create a dashboard that displays the CPU usage, memory usage, and network traffic for each Kubernetes cluster, allowing you to quickly identify any performance issues.

Summary

We discussed the topic of multi-cloud CI/CD and its importance in modern software development. We started by defining the concept of multi-cloud CI/CD, which involves using multiple cloud platforms to build, test, and deploy software applications.

To set up a multi-cloud CI/CD pipeline, we recommended using Jenkins, an open-source automation server that can be easily integrated with different cloud providers. We highlighted the benefits of using Jenkins, including its ability to automate the software delivery process, support for various programming languages and tools, and its rich plugin ecosystem.

We then discussed the deployment of applications across multiple clusters, which involves distributing application workloads across different cloud environments. We noted that the key to achieving this successfully is to adopt a containerized approach to software development, which enables developers to build and package applications once and run them anywhere.

We also emphasized the importance of managing configuration and secrets when deploying applications in multi-cloud environments. We recommended using tools like Kubernetes ConfigMaps and Secrets to store configuration data and sensitive information securely, while making them easily accessible to the application at runtime.

Finally, we discussed the importance of testing and monitoring in multi-cloud CI/CD. We highlighted the challenges of testing and monitoring in a distributed environment and recommended using tools like Prometheus and Grafana to collect and visualize data across multiple cloud environments.

CHAPTER 8: SECURITY IN MULTI-CLOUD KUBERNETES

Introduction to Kubernetes Security

The necessity of Kubernetes security stems from the fact that Kubernetes is a complex system that manages critical infrastructure and applications running in production environments. As such, Kubernetes clusters are potential targets for attackers who may attempt to gain unauthorized access, steal sensitive data, or disrupt critical services. Kubernetes security is necessary to protect against these threats and ensure the confidentiality, integrity, and availability of Kubernetes resources.

Need of Kubernetes Security

Protection against attacks: Kubernetes security helps to protect Kubernetes clusters against attacks from external and internal sources. This includes protecting against denial-of-service (DoS) attacks, man-in-the-middle (MITM) attacks, and other types of attacks that can compromise Kubernetes resources.

Compliance: Many industries and organizations have regulatory compliance requirements that must be met to protect sensitive data. Kubernetes security can help to ensure compliance with these regulations by providing features such as RBAC, network policies, and secrets management.

Data protection: Kubernetes security helps to protect sensitive data such as passwords, API keys, and certificates from unauthorized access and exposure. This is important for protecting the confidentiality and integrity of data stored in Kubernetes resources.

Business continuity: Kubernetes security is necessary for ensuring the availability of Kubernetes resources and preventing service disruptions. This is critical for business continuity and preventing revenue loss due to downtime or service disruptions.

Reputation management: Security breaches can damage the reputation of an organization and erode trust with customers and partners. Kubernetes security is necessary for protecting the reputation of organizations that rely on Kubernetes for managing critical applications and infrastructure.

Kubernetes security is a critical aspect of deploying and managing applications on Kubernetes. Kubernetes provides a range of security features and best practices to help protect Kubernetes clusters and the applications running on them from security threats and vulnerabilities.

Authentication and Authorization

One of the biggest security challenges in a multi-cloud Kubernetes environment is managing authentication and authorization across multiple clusters and cloud providers. It's important to ensure that only authorized users and services can access your Kubernetes resources.

To address this challenge, you can use Kubernetes RBAC (Role-Based Access Control) to define roles and permissions for users and services. You can also use tools like OIDC (OpenID Connect) to manage authentication and SSO (Single Sign-On) across multiple Kubernetes clusters.

Network Security

Another important security challenge in a multi-cloud Kubernetes environment is securing the network communication between Kubernetes clusters and cloud providers. It's important to ensure that your network traffic is encrypted and that your Kubernetes clusters are isolated from each other and from the public internet.

To address this challenge, you can use Kubernetes network policies to define rules for incoming and outgoing network traffic. You can also use tools like Istio to manage service mesh and encrypt network traffic between Kubernetes clusters.

Data Security

Data security is another important concern in a multi-cloud Kubernetes environment. It's important to ensure that your sensitive data is protected from unauthorized access and that your data is encrypted both at rest and in transit.

To address this challenge, you can use Kubernetes secrets to manage sensitive data like passwords and API keys. You can also use tools like Vault to manage and encrypt secrets across multiple Kubernetes clusters.

Compliance

Finally, compliance is an important concern in a multi-cloud Kubernetes environment. You need to ensure that your Kubernetes clusters and applications comply with various security and privacy regulations like GDPR, HIPAA, and PCI DSS.

To address this challenge, you can use tools like Open Policy Agent to define policies for compliance and security. You can also use tools like Falco to detect and prevent security violations and policy violations in real-time.

To sum up, a multi-cloud Kubernetes environment poses various security challenges, including authentication and authorization, network security, data security, and compliance. To address these challenges, you can use Kubernetes RBAC, network policies, secrets management, compliance tools, and security tools like Falco to secure your environment.

Using RBAC for Authentication and Authorization

Below is a practical example of how to use Kubernetes RBAC (Role-Based Access Control) to define roles and permissions for users and services in a multi-cloud Kubernetes environment:

Define Roles and Role Bindings

First, define the roles and role bindings that you want to use to control access to your Kubernetes resources. For example, you might define a viewer role that allows users to view resources, but not modify them, and a developer role that allows users to create and modify resources.

Below is an example viewer role manifest:

```
apiVersion: rbac.authorization.k8s.io/v1
kind: Role
metadata:
  name: viewer
rules:
- apiGroups: ["", "apps", "batch"]
  resources: ["pods", "replicationcontrollers", "services", "deployments", "jobs", "cronjobs"]
  verbs: ["get", "list", "watch"]
```

In the above demonstrated example, we define a role named viewer that grants users read access to pods, replication controllers, services, deployments, jobs, and cron jobs.

Next, define a role binding that associates the viewer role with a specific user or group. For example:

```yaml
apiVersion: rbac.authorization.k8s.io/v1
kind: RoleBinding
metadata:
  name: viewer-binding
subjects:
- kind: User
  name: alice
  apiGroup: rbac.authorization.k8s.io
roleRef:
  kind: Role
  name: viewer
  apiGroup: rbac.authorization.k8s.io
```

In the above demonstrated example, we define a role binding named viewer-binding that associates the viewer role with the user alice.

Apply Roles and Role Bindings

Next, apply the roles and role bindings to your Kubernetes clusters using kubectl apply command. For example:

```
$ kubectl apply -f viewer-role.yaml
$ kubectl apply -f viewer-role-binding.yaml
```

This will create the viewer role and the viewer-binding role binding in your Kubernetes clusters.

Verify Access

Finally, verify that the roles and role bindings are working as expected by trying to access the resources that the viewer role allows. For example, if you have a pod named myapp in your Kubernetes cluster, you can use the kubectl get pods command to verify that the user alice can view the pod:

```
$ kubectl config set-context --current --user=alice
$ kubectl get pods
```

This should return a list of pods in your Kubernetes cluster, including the myapp pod.

By following these steps, you can use Kubernetes RBAC to define roles and permissions for users and services in a multi-cloud Kubernetes environment, and control access to your Kubernetes resources.

Using Kubernetes Network Policies

Let us see how to use Kubernetes network policies to define rules for incoming and outgoing network traffic:

Enable Network Policies

First, you need to ensure that network policies are enabled in your Kubernetes clusters. Network policies are not enabled by default, so you need to enable them by setting the NetworkPolicy feature gate to true when you start your Kubernetes control plane.

Below is an example of how to start a Kubernetes control plane with network policies enabled:

```
$ kubeadm init --pod-network-cidr=10.244.0.0/16 --feature-gates=NetworkPolicy=true
```

Define Network Policies

Next, define the network policies that you want to use to control network traffic in your Kubernetes clusters. For example, you might define a policy that allows traffic only from specific pods or namespaces, or a policy that blocks traffic to specific ports or IP ranges.

Below is an example allow-from-namespace network policy manifest that allows traffic only from pods in a specific namespace:

```
apiVersion: networking.k8s.io/v1
kind: NetworkPolicy
metadata:
  name: allow-from-namespace
spec:
  podSelector: {}
```

```yaml
policyTypes:
- Ingress
ingress:
- from:
  - namespaceSelector:
    matchLabels:
      name: my-namespace
```

In the above demonstrated example, we define a network policy named allow-from-namespace that allows ingress traffic only from pods in the my-namespace namespace.

Below is another example deny-http network policy manifest that blocks traffic to HTTP ports:

```yaml
apiVersion: networking.k8s.io/v1
kind: NetworkPolicy
metadata:
  name: deny-http
spec:
  podSelector: {}
  policyTypes:
  - Ingress
  ingress:
  - from: []
    ports:
    - protocol: TCP
      port: 80
```

In the above demonstrated example, we define a network policy named deny-http that blocks ingress traffic to the HTTP port (port 80).

Apply Network Policies

Next, apply the network policies to your Kubernetes clusters using kubectl apply command. For example:

```
$ kubectl apply -f allow-from-namespace.yaml
$ kubectl apply -f deny-http.yaml
```

This will create the allow-from-namespace and deny-http network policies in your Kubernetes clusters.

Verify Network Policies

Finally, verify that the network policies are working as expected by trying to access your pods and services from different pods or namespaces. You can use the kubectl describe networkpolicy command to view the details of your network policies and check which traffic is allowed or blocked.

For example, if you have a pod named myapp that listens on port 8080 in your Kubernetes cluster, you can try to access it from another pod or namespace to verify that the network policies are working:

```
$ kubectl run --rm -it --image=alpine:latest test-pod -- sh
/ # wget --timeout=2 -qO- http://myapp:8080
```

If the deny-http network policy is applied, this should return an error message indicating that the connection was refused.

By following these steps, you can use Kubernetes network policies to define rules for incoming and outgoing network traffic in a multi-cloud Kubernetes environment, and control access to your pods and services.

Manage Data Security with Kubernetes Secrets

We will now see how to use Kubernetes secrets to manage sensitive data like passwords and API keys:

Define the Secret

First, define the secret that you want to use to store your sensitive data. For example, you might define a secret named db-credentials that contains the username and password for your database.

Below is an example db-credentials secret manifest:

```yaml
apiVersion: v1
kind: Secret
metadata:
  name: db-credentials
type: Opaque
data:
  username: <base64-encoded-username>
  password: <base64-encoded-password>
```

In the above demonstrated example, we define a secret named db-credentials that contains the username and password fields, each base64-encoded.

Apply the Secret

Next, apply the secret to your Kubernetes cluster using kubectl apply command. For example:

```
$ kubectl apply -f db-credentials.yaml
```

This will create the db-credentials secret in your Kubernetes cluster.

Use the Secret

Finally, use the secret in your Kubernetes manifests to retrieve the sensitive data. For example, if you have a deployment that needs access to the database, you can use the envFrom field in the deployment manifest to load the db-credentials secret as environment variables.

Below is an example deployment manifest that uses the db-credentials secret:

```yaml
apiVersion: apps/v1
kind: Deployment
metadata:
  name: myapp
```

```yaml
spec:
 replicas: 1
 selector:
  matchLabels:
   app: myapp
 template:
  metadata:
   labels:
    app: myapp
  spec:
   containers:
   - name: myapp
     image: myapp:latest
     envFrom:
     - secretRef:
        name: db-credentials
```

In the above demonstrated example, we define a deployment named myapp that loads the db-credentials secret as environment variables.

Once the deployment is running, you can access the sensitive data using the environment variables. For example, you might retrieve the database credentials in your application code using os.environ['DB_USERNAME'] and os.environ['DB_PASSWORD'].

By following these steps, you can use Kubernetes secrets to manage sensitive data like passwords and API keys in a multi-cloud Kubernetes environment, and securely access the sensitive data from your applications.

Use Open Policy Agent for Compliance

Let us try to use Open Policy Agent (OPA) to define policies for compliance and security of a multi-cloud Kubernetes environment:

Install OPA

First, install OPA in your Kubernetes cluster. You can use the OPA Helm chart to install

OPA, or you can install it manually using the OPA Kubernetes manifest.

Below is an example of how to install OPA using the Helm chart:

```
$ helm repo add open-policy-agent https://open-policy-agent.github.io/charts
$ helm install opa open-policy-agent/opa
```

Define Policies

Next, define the policies that you want to enforce using OPA. OPA uses a policy language called Rego that allows you to define policies in a declarative way.

For example, you might define a policy that requires all containers to run with a non-root user, or a policy that requires all Kubernetes objects to have labels that conform to a specific format.

Below is an example non-root-user policy that requires all containers to run with a non-root user:

```
package kubernetes.admission

deny[msg] {
    input.request.kind.kind == "Pod"
    container := input.request.object.spec.containers[_]
    container.securityContext.runAsUser == 0
    msg := sprintf("container %v in pod %v running as root", [container.name,
input.request.object.metadata.name])
}
```

In the above demonstrated example, we define a policy that denies any pod that has a container running as root.

Deploy Policies

Next, deploy the policies to your Kubernetes cluster using the OPA Kubernetes manifest. You can use the configMap and service resources in the manifest to define your policies and enable the OPA admission controller.

Below is an example of how to deploy the non-root-user policy using the OPA Kubernetes manifest:

```yaml
apiVersion: v1
kind: ConfigMap
metadata:
  name: opa-policy
data:
 kubernetes.admission.rego: |
   package kubernetes.admission

   deny[msg] {
     input.request.kind.kind == "Pod"
     container := input.request.object.spec.containers[_]
     container.securityContext.runAsUser == 0
     msg := sprintf("container %v in pod %v running as root", [container.name,
input.request.object.metadata.name])
   }

---
apiVersion: apps/v1
kind: Deployment
metadata:
  name: opa
spec:
 selector:
  matchLabels:
    app: opa
 replicas: 1
 template:
  metadata:
   labels:
```

```yaml
    app: opa
  spec:
   containers:
    - name: opa
      image: openpolicyagent/opa:latest
      args:
       - "run"
       - "--server"
       - "--config-file=/app/config.yaml"
       - "--addr=:8181"
      ports:
       - containerPort: 8181
      volumeMounts:
       - name: config
         mountPath: /app/config.yaml
         subPath: config.yaml
    volumes:
     - name: config
       configMap:
        name: opa-policy
```

In the above demonstrated example, we define a ConfigMap named opa-policy that contains the non-root-user policy. We also define a deployment that runs the OPA server and mounts the ConfigMap as a file.

Verify Policies

Finally, verify that the policies are working as expected by creating or updating Kubernetes objects that should be denied by the policies. OPA will deny any objects that violate the policies and provide a detailed error message.

For example, if you create a pod with a container running as root, OPA should deny the pod creation and provide an error message that explains why the pod was denied.

You can use the kubectl command to create or update Kubernetes objects and see the OPA response. For example:

```
$ kubectl apply -f my-pod.yaml
```

If the pod contains a container running as root, OPA should deny the pod creation and provide an error message.

By following these steps, you can use Open Policy Agent (OPA) to define policies for compliance and security of a multi-cloud Kubernetes environment, and ensure that your Kubernetes objects comply with the policies.

Summary

In this chapter, we covered various aspects of security in a multi-cloud Kubernetes environment, including the challenges of securing such an environment, and various techniques for securing Kubernetes clusters, such as using RBAC, network policies, secrets, and Open Policy Agent (OPA).

One of the key challenges of securing a multi-cloud Kubernetes environment is the need to manage security across multiple clouds and Kubernetes clusters, which can introduce complexity and increase the attack surface. To address this challenge, it's important to use a layered approach to security, including both network-level and application-level security measures.

RBAC is a Kubernetes feature that allows you to define roles and permissions for users and services, which can help to control access to Kubernetes resources and reduce the risk of unauthorized access. By defining RBAC rules for your Kubernetes clusters, you can ensure that only authorized users and services have access to sensitive data and resources.

Network policies are another Kubernetes feature that allows you to define rules for incoming and outgoing network traffic, which can help to control access to your Kubernetes resources and reduce the risk of network-based attacks. By defining network policies for your Kubernetes clusters, you can ensure that only authorized traffic is allowed to and from your Kubernetes resources.

Kubernetes secrets are used to manage sensitive data like passwords and API keys. By storing sensitive data in secrets, you can ensure that it's securely stored and only accessible by authorized users and services.

Open Policy Agent (OPA) is a policy engine that allows you to define policies for compliance and security of your Kubernetes resources. By defining policies in OPA, you can ensure that your Kubernetes resources comply with security and compliance standards, and reduce the risk of security breaches.

In summary, securing a multi-cloud Kubernetes environment requires a layered approach to security, including RBAC, network policies, secrets, and OPA. By implementing these techniques, you can ensure that your Kubernetes clusters are secure and compliant with industry standards, and reduce the risk of security breaches and unauthorized access to your resources.

Thank You

Epilogue

As you close the last page of "Hands-On Multi-Cloud Kubernetes," you reflect on the journey you've taken to get here. Eight chapters of comprehensive and hands-on learning have brought you from a beginner's understanding of Kubernetes to a skilled practitioner capable of managing and deploying multi-cloud infrastructure.

You recall the beginning of your journey, where you learned the basics of setting up a Kubernetes cluster and managing infrastructure using various tools. From there, you delved into the intricacies of working with AWS and GCP, becoming proficient in administering deployments and updates across multiple cloud environments.

As you continued through the book, you were introduced to a range of powerful tools, including Helm, FluxCD, Virtual Kubelet, Submariner, and KubeFed. With each new tool, you gained a deeper understanding of Kubernetes and how it can be used to manage complex multi-cloud infrastructure.

With GitOps principles and workflows, you learned how to practice continuous delivery and manage secrets and config maps. You built and deployed serverless clusters using Virtual Kubelet and learned to scale them across multiple cloud environments. You were even introduced to the world of cross-cluster networking with Submariner, where you learned to perform service discovery, load balancing, and monitor networking metrics.

Managing multi-cluster Kubernetes can be a daunting task, but with KubeFed, you gained the skills necessary to set up and deploy multicluster federation, making it easier than ever to administer your own infrastructure. And with multi-cloud CI/CD pipelines using Jenkins, you performed end-to-end multi-cloud operations, ensuring your code was delivered quickly and efficiently.

Finally, the book covered security in Kubernetes, giving you the tools and knowledge to configure RBAC, Kubernetes network policies, and securing data over Kubernetes clusters. You even learned to use Open Policy Agent for managing compliance, ensuring that your infrastructure was both powerful and secure.

As you reflect on your journey through "Hands-On Multi-Cloud Kubernetes," you feel a sense of pride and accomplishment. The knowledge and skills you have gained will undoubtedly serve you well in your future endeavors, both personally and professionally. With your newfound understanding of Kubernetes and multi-cloud infrastructure, you can confidently take on any challenge that comes your way.

As you close the book for the last time, you feel a sense of excitement about what lies ahead. The world of Kubernetes and multi-cloud infrastructure is constantly evolving, and you look forward to continuing your journey of discovery and learning. With the knowledge and skills you've gained from this book, you know that you are ready to take on whatever the future may hold.

Made in the USA
Monee, IL
07 July 2026

56552389R00096